WOMEN TO THE RESCUE

ISBN 1-887805-14-1

Author
Duane A. Smith

Mesa Verde Centennial Series Editor
Andrew Gulliford

Copy Editor
Elizabeth A. Green

Design and Layout
Lisa Snider Atchison

Printed in Korea

For

A Dear, Longtime Friend

And Southwestern Historian/Archaeologist

Florence Lister

A message from the Superintendent of Mesa Verde National Park

Our centennial celebrates an important moment in Mesa Verde National Park's history. It is an opportunity to share stories of what led to establishment of the park on June 29, 1906, and its designation as a World Heritage Cultural Site in 1978. This is a time to reflect upon its past and share hopes and visions for the next 100 years.

As Mesa Verde National Park nears its 100th birthday, it is important to remember that the archaeological sites it protects have been here far longer. Their survival is a credit to the skilled Ancestral Puebloan masons who created them 700 to 1600 years ago.

Following the Puebloan people's migration south to the Rio Grande area around 1300, the Utes continued to occupy the Mesa Verde area. They remain today and were responsible for the protection and preservation of Mesa Verde prior to its establishment as a national park. The park and the American public owe much to all these surviving indigenous people.

More than 100 years before its establishment as a national park, non-native people began exploring and documenting the archaeological sites at Mesa Verde, including Spanish explorers, geologists, ranchers, miners, photographers, naturalists, and archaeologists. They shared the story of fantastic stone cities in the cliffs, attracting more and more visitors to the area.

Prior to 1914, the 25-mile trek from Mancos Canyon to Spruce Tree House took an entire day, traveling the first 15 miles by wagon and the next 10 miles on foot or by horseback. This included a nearly vertical climb to the top of Chapin Mesa. Today more than one-half million people visit Mesa Verde National Park each year—a considerable increase over the 100 visitors documented in 1906.

"Leaving the past in place" is just one of the unique ideas pioneered at Mesa Verde. In 1908, when archaeology mainly consisted of collecting artifacts for distant museums, Jesse Walter Fewkes repaired, but did not rebuild, Spruce Tree House for visitation. He documented the excavation and created a small museum to house its artifacts. That tradition is continued today and Mesa Verde is recognized worldwide as a leader in non-invasive archaeology—studying and documenting sites without shovels to disturb the past. With the involvement of the 24 tribes affiliated with Mesa Verde and ongoing research, we continue to learn more about the stories that Mesa Verde National Park preserves.

Our centennial will celebrate 100 years of preservation and honor all who have gone before us. This centennial book series was created to tell some of their stories, of discovery, travel, transportation, archaeology, fire and tourism. These stories have contributed to our national heritage and reinforce why we must continue to preserve and protect this national treasure for future generations.

Enjoy the celebration. Enjoy the book series. Enjoy your national park.

About the Mesa Verde Museum Association

Mesa Verde Museum Association (MVMA) is a nonprofit, 501 (c) 3 organization, authorized by Congress, established in 1930, and incorporated in 1960. MVMA was the second "cooperating association" formed in the United States after the Yosemite Association. Since its inception, the museum association has provided information that enables visitors to more fully appreciate the cultural and natural resources in Mesa Verde National Park and the southwestern United States. Working under a memorandum of agreement with the National Park Service, the association assists and supports various research activities, interpretive and education programs, and visitor services at Mesa Verde National Park.

A Board of Directors sets policy and provides guidance for the association. An Executive Director assures mission goals are met, strengthens partnerships, and manages publishing, education, and membership program development. A small year-round staff of five, along with more than 15 seasonal employees, operates four sales outlets in Mesa Verde National Park and a bookstore in Cortez, Colorado. The association carries nearly 600 items, the majority of which are produced by outside vendors. MVMA currently publishes approximately 40 books, videos, and theme-related items, and more than 15 trail guides.

Since 1996 MVMA has been a charter partner in the Plateau Journal, a semi-annual interpretive journal covering the people and places of the Colorado Plateau. In addition, the association has been a driving force in the Peaks, Plateaus & Canyons Association (PPCA), a region-wide conference of nonprofit interpretive associations. PPCA promotes understanding and protection of the Colorado Plateau through the publication of joint projects that are not feasible for smaller associations.

Mesa Verde Museum Association is also a longtime member of the Association of Partners for Public Lands (APPL). This national organization of non-profit interpretive associations provides national representation with our land management partners and highly specialized training opportunities for board and staff.

Since 1930 the association has donated more than $2 million in cash contributions, interpretive services, and educational material to Mesa Verde National Park. MVMA's goal is to continue enhancing visitor experience through its products and services, supporting vital park programs in interpretation, research and education.

Visit the on-line bookstore at mesaverde.org and learn more about Mesa Verde National Park's centennial celebration at mesaverde2006.org. Contact MVMA offices for additional information at: telephone 970-529-4445; write P.O. Box 38, Mesa Verde National Park, CO 81330; or email info@mesaverde.org.

The Center of Southwest Studies

The Center of Southwest Studies on the campus of Fort Lewis College in Durango, Colorado serves as a museum and a research facility, hosts public programs, and strengthen an interdisciplinary Southwest college curriculum. Fort Lewis College offers a four-year degree in Southwest Studies with minors in Native American Studies and Heritage Preservation. The Center includes a 4,400-square-foot gallery, the Robert Delaney Research Library, a 100-seat lyceum, and more than 10,000 square feet of collections storage. The new $8 million Center of Southwest Studies building is unique among four-year public colleges in the West, because the facility houses the departments of Southwest Studies and Anthropology, and the Office of Community Services, which helps Four Corners communities with historic preservation and cultural resource planning.

The Colorado Commission on Higher Education has recognized the Center of Southwest Studies as a "program of excellence" in state-funded higher education. Recent gifts to the Center include the $2.5 million Durango Collection ®, which features more than eight hundred years of Southwestern weavings from Pueblo, Navajo and Hispanic cultures.

The goal of the Center is to become the intellectual heart of Durango and the Southwest and to provide a variety of educational and research opportunities for students, residents, scholars and visitors. Strengths in the Center's collections of artifacts include Ancestral Puebloan ceramic vessels, more than 500 textiles and dozens of Southwestern baskets. The Center's holdings, which focus on the Four Corners region, include more than 8,000 artifacts, 20,000 volumes, numerous periodicals, and 500 special collections dating from prehistory to the present and with an emphasis on southwestern archaeology, maps, and original documents. These collections include nearly two linear miles of manuscripts, unbound printed materials, more than 7,000 rolls of microfilm (including about 3,000 rolls of historic Southwest region newspapers), 600 oral histories, and 200,000 photographs. Contact the Center at 970-247-7456 or visit the Center's website at swcenter.fortlewis.edu. The Center hosts tours, educational programs, a speakers' series, and changing exhibits throughout the year.

Center of SW Studies website: http://swcenter.fortlewis.edu

About the publisher

The publisher for the Mesa Verde Centennial Series is the Ballantine family of Durango and the Durango Herald Small Press. The Ballantine family moved to the Four Corners region in 1952 when it purchased the *Durango Herald* newspaper.

Durango has a magnificent setting, close to the Continental Divide, the 13,000-foot San Juan Mountains, and the 500,000-acre Weminuche Wilderness. The Four Corners region encompasses the juncture of Colorado, Utah, Arizona, and New Mexico, the only place in the nation where four state borders meet. Residents can choose to ski one day in the San Juans and hike the next day in the wilderness canyons of southeast Utah. This land of mountains and canyons, deserts and rivers is home to diverse Native American tribes including the Southern Utes, Ute Mountain Utes, Jicarilla Apache, Hopi, Zuni, and the Navajo, whose 17 million-acre nation sprawls across all four states. The Four Corners is situated on the edge of the Colorado Plateau, which has more national forests, national parks, national monuments, and wilderness areas than anywhere else on earth.

Writing and editing the newspaper launched countless family expeditions to Ancestral Puebloan sites in the area, including spectacular Mesa Verde National Park, the world's first park set aside for the preservation of cultural resources in 1906 to honor America's indigenous peoples. The Ballantine family, through the *Durango Herald* and the *Cortez Journal,* have been strong supporters of Mesa Verde National Park and Fort Lewis College.

Arthur and Morley Ballantine started the planning for the Center of Southwest Studies at Fort Lewis College in 1964 with a $10,000 gift. In 1994 Morley began the Durango Herald Small Press, which publishes books of local and regional interest. The Press is proud to be a part of the 100th birthday celebration for Mesa Verde National Park.

Durango Herald Small Press website: www.theheraldstore.com

TABLE OF CONTENTS

PREFACE

The June 1972 *Arizona Highways* enticed readers to come to Colorado in an article by Joyce Rockwood entitled, "What's Up in Colorado."

A ten-day safari into southwestern Colorado can be an eye-opener if this is your first visit, a welcome refresher if you have gone before. The route, arrayed as the old saying prescribes for the bride, offers "something old" in jewel-like, ancient cities built centuries ago; "something new" with ski resorts as fresh as last night's powder snow . . .

This is a story about those ancient cities that intrigued so many writers long before Rockwood's article appeared. Those earlier authors, too, tried to find words to describe the scenery and those "jewel-like" cities.

Denver newspaperwoman Margaret Keating tackled the problem back in the October 1907 issue of *The Modern World,* when Mesa Verde National Park was moving into its second year. Keating's article opened with a poem by Lida Frowe.

> Cliffs of the Mancos, frowning and sullen
> Deep in thy hollows strange secrets abide;
> Once thou wert home for a long-buried people
> Now in thy fastness the wild beasts abide.

Then Keating eulogized:

> The story of an extinct people is written upon the walls of the deserted dwellings of Mesa Verde, but we have failed to interpret the handwriting. The Mesa Verde, immortalized by the relics of its unknown inhabitants, is a region of international interest, and the revelations of its secrets are of deep import in the world of science and letters, touching, as they do, the history of an ancient race.

Appropriately, women wrote all of these words, because Mesa Verde's early history is the saga of turn-of-the-century women who ventured forth to save the remains of an epoch in American history.

This national park became a national and a world treasure, and its history has been told numerous times. Yet in that telling, not all the people involved have received their fair share of credit. Women led the fight to educate the public and to preserve the wonderful treasures that became Mesa Verde National Park. They did this at a time when women were supposed to stay at home and not venture beyond their families. History has not been kind to them, and too often their contributions have received only a passing acknowledgment.

Keating knew and appreciated what the women did. She hailed their efforts—they "neither slumbered nor slept," and they gave of their time, talents, strength, and money. Still a sadness is inherent in all this, for it was not posterity that pushed these women to the historical sidelines. The women themselves carry most of the blame. This, then, is their story, the story of the preservation and creation of Mesa Verde National Park.

An author owes a deep debt of gratitude to many people for their encouragement, help, and support, and I am no exception. My sincere thanks to Tracey Chavis, her staff, and the Mesa Verde Museum Association. Without Tracey and Mesa Verde Historic Monograph Editorial Committee, there would have been no series honoring Mesa Verde's 100th birthday. This book is a part of that series. As usual, Todd Ellison and his efficient staff in the Southwest Center Library at Fort Lewis College provided invaluable assistance.

The staffs of the Denver Public Library Western History Department, Durango Public Library, and the Colorado Historical Society lent their expertise. Three cheers to Cheryl Carnahan, who did her usual professional editing with enthusiasm and insightfulness. I also owe a great debt of gratitude to Liz Bauer for her assistance in the Mesa Verde National Park Archives. Lisa Atchison was very helpful in creating the finished product with her variety of layout and publishing skills.

As usual my wife Gay worked with me and encouraged me throughout in the process of turning ideas into words. Her love and support are the keystone in all my literary efforts.

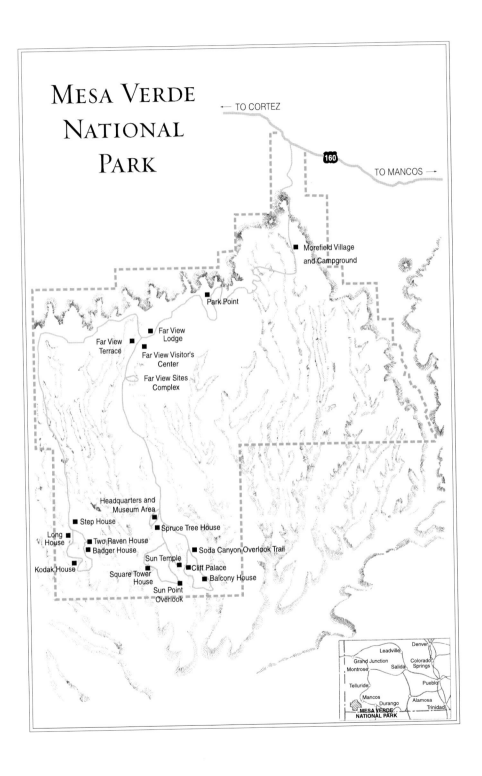

"The Mothers
of
Mesa Verde"

T he visitor to Mesa Verde National Park, unless well-informed or a careful student of everything she or he sees and reads, will not know why or how the park came into existence. Neither will park visitors gain an understanding of who motivated and guided the movement to save what modern visitors so appreciate and are grateful to see. Who preserved and protected this fascinating cultural heritage? We owe a tremendous debt of gratitude to these nearly forgotten people. It is a sad commentary on the times and, unfortunately, on the "movers" themselves, that women have been virtually neglected in the history of the park and their fight forgotten.

Denver Public Library

Virginia Donaghe McClurg ca. 1880.

Betty Friedan asked in the 1960s, "Who knows what women can be when they are finally free to become themselves?" In a sense, Margaret Mead later answered that question: "Women have a special contribution to make to any group enterprise, and I feel it is up to them to contribute the kinds of awareness that relatively few men . . . have incorporated through their education."

Two women answered Friedan's question and supported Mead's assertion nearly seventy-five years before either of them wrote. In the late nineteenth century, Virginia Donaghe McClurg and Lucy Peabody, along with the women they recruited and gathered together, showed that determination, dedication, perseverance, ability, and a never-say-die spirit could overcome a variety of obstacles and lead to success. Their accomplishments? They preserved the ruins at Mesa Verde and were instrumental in creating a national park—the first park in the world to preserve a cultural heritage.

Elizabeth Dole expressed a further desire: "Women share with men the need for personal success, even the taste for power, and no longer are willing to satisfy those needs through the achievement of surrogates, whether husbands, children or merely role models." McClurg and Peabody clearly displayed that need and proved without question to have the capability, fortitude, and motivation to succeed with a daunting project filled with a minefield of troubles and trials.

One might not have expected such effort from McClurg and Peabody, considering their typical middle-class, Protestant, Victorian backgrounds. Neither woman, however, should be considered a typical Victorian woman in the sense of limiting herself to being a wife and mother confined to the home.

Mary Virginia Donaghe McClurg was born in New York City in 1858 and was educated in Virginia. "Such irregular education as she ever received—though the dull drudgery of the school-room was never for her." Like so many she came West, arriving in Colorado in 1879 as a teacher at a private school and a correspondent for several newspapers. Fairly quickly, she dropped the names Mary and M. Donaghe, and settled on Virginia Donaghe.

Her goal as a reporter became covering southwestern Colorado—Durango and Mancos because of their nearness to the cliff ruins—and the buildings of the "ancient" peoples about whom she had heard. Already fascinated by what she had read, McClurg became captivated by the ruins that had been found in Mancos Canyon. She wrote about what she saw (as she described them, "Colorado's wonderful buried cities and lost homes"), as well as writing other western stories. The enthusiastic Coloradan contributed articles to, among others, *Review of Reviews*, *Cosmopolitan*, and *Century*, and she also wrote for a Colorado Springs newspaper. McClurg additionally wrote poetry and published a book of illustrated poems, *Seven Sonnets of Sculpture*, as well as pamphlets eulogizing the "scenic West" and Colorado. The homes of the ancient people, however, became her lifelong passion. She had found a cause.

Her most detailed accounts appeared in a series of 1889 articles in the *Great Divide*, published in Denver. James MacCarthy, or as he was better known to his readers, "Fitz-Mac," described McClurg in a sketch as belonging to "our gang," a "clever and accomplished journalist." Further, "She is an incomparable cook and housekeeper, and can make a pot-pie as well as a poem. Her energy is tireless." Fitz-Mac concluded about his obvious friend: "In her home she receives a circle of friends with all that easy charm and distinction of presence which in the last generation marked the hospitalities of the old McClurg aristocracy."

Although she used fictitious characters to tell her story, as Fitz-Mac told his readers, McClurg's enthusiasm and excitement came through abundantly. To her, exploring southwestern Colorado was like going into the "frontier," which was "fast passing away." This "picturesque region" included Durango, "our outfitting point, [which] is, as one of its pioneers has left on record with charming candor, 'the most unrelicky place on the globe'." With flowery Victorian prose, McClurg chronicled her own (she is the "Enthusiast") and "her friends" adventures. It seems more logical, however, that she used "fictitious" names for real people, not fictitious people:

"To our dust-dried throats it was nectar [claret mixed with sugar, lemon juice, and "muddy Rio" Mancos water]. We partook and chatted and rested and eventually writing our names on a piece of paper inserted it in the [claret] bottle and buried the latter deeply in a locality we had christened the 'goat corral.'

"The afternoon was wearing away when galloping hoofs announced friends or foes, and half a dozen cowboys with cartridge belts and jingling spurs draw rein and stare with unaffected surprise at the ladies. The [Cliff Dwellers'] decoration is simple, chaste and artistic, and everyone

Lucy Peabody ca. late 19-teens.

of the circling, parallel lines is clear and true. 'The Enthusiast' forgot her ailing, aching body . . . She rises, reels, staggers over Mrs. Van's corner [who had just found a 'perfect' jar], and throwing herself down by the rubbish pile essays to dig.

"[The Enthusiast also enjoyed describing the scenery.] When the perils are over, and the canon widens into a vista of sun-flecked verdant, arches, where 'blue aisles of heaven laugh between,' . . .

"But however mysteriously harassed and even denied a foothold on the earth, till they perched in eagle-like eyries—their religion, their superstition—term it as you will, demanded that the state estufa tower should rise with undiminished proportions, its stones nearly laid to the curve, and wherever they could [build] a home they must also rear a temple."

After her marriage to Gilbert McClurg in 1889, the couple resided in Colorado Springs. He proved very supportive, encouraging her interests and activities in southwestern Colorado. Both of them became well-known in the city as writers, lecturers, and historians—she more than he. Her crusade to save the Mesa Verde ruins brought her recognition statewide and nationally. McClurg's organizational abilities, her passion for the "ancient" peoples, and her writing and speaking expertise proved invaluable to the cause.

Lucy Peabody, born in Cincinnati in 1863, was educated there and in Washington, D.C. While in the nation's capital, Peabody became interested in ethnology. She worked as a secretarial assistant at the Bureau of American Ethnology for nine years and became an advocate for and involved in the movement to preserve ancient cliff ruins. Her affiliation with the Bureau and its officials paid huge dividends during the "struggle." Not all her time was spent researching and working. She met and fell in love with her future husband, Major William Peabody, while he was stationed in Washington. After he retired from the army, they moved to his home state of Colorado in the 1880s and established residence in the state's capital city, Denver. His brother, Canon City merchant James Peabody, later was Colorado's controversial governor during an apex of labor troubles in 1903-04, turmoil that coincided with the last years of the fight to save Mesa Verde.

"Gifted and charming," Peabody knew her way around Washington's politics, a valued asset in the decade-long struggle over what to do with the Mesa Verde cliff dwellings. Described as a "cultured woman," who "has made extensive research into archaeology and anthropology," she would work and lobby untiringly in both Denver and Washington. She "gave her time, strength, and money" to preserve Mesa Verde.

"No woman in the country has a more thorough and profound knowledge of Archaeology, Anthropology and Ethnology, than this earnest, able, enthusiastic student of scientific research," wrote one ardent admirer. Nor was this praise alone. After the creation of the park, the American Anthropological Association passed its first public vote of thanks "ever tended anyone" to Lucy Peabody for her "exceptionally noteworthy service to science." It continued, the "accomplishment of this object was due in great measure to [her] untiring effort."

Peabody not only wrote articles advocating the cause. She contributed two important elements to the crusade—her interest in and enthusiasm for ethnology and cliff dwellings and her Washington experience. Peabody left "no stone unturned to make the work of the Association successful." Not stopping there, she was secretary of the Archaeological Society and also served as a member of the Archaeological Institute of America's legislative committee. Ever modest, she disclaimed being a "scientist" or archaeologist, but as her friends noted, she was "well versed in cliff-dwelling lore."

Notwithstanding being involved in the struggle to preserve Mesa Verde, Peabody remained active in other "crusades." This "quiet little woman," as newspaper reporter Lillian Hartman described her, "never yet met defeat in any of the measures she has started out to champion."

She fought for and succeeded in getting passed through the legislature a bill creating a Traveling Library Commission. This was "the first bill that the women of Colorado ever got through the legislature carrying an appropriation with it. They asked for $2,000, but secured $1,000 a year." She also worked as deputy registrar in the State Land Office both during and after her involvement with the creation of the park.

"In the same year [1903], Lincoln's birthday was made a legal holiday in the state, largely through the efforts of Mrs. Peabody, who secured the measure as an amendment to a bill making the holidays of the West uniform." Colorado thus became the ninth state to make that day a holiday. Lincoln was apparently a great favorite of Peabody's: "One of the most valuable collections in the United States of Lincoln data is owned by Mrs. Peabody." She began as a young girl collecting books, pictures, and "relics of great value."

Peabody later worked on behalf of juvenile court bills; thanks to reformer Ben Lindsey and supporters like Peabody, Colorado led the nation in establishing juvenile courts. Hartman complimented her with this observation: "The women of Colorado owe much to Mrs. Peabody for the work she did to get the child labor law through the legislature." Hartman continued, "In a quiet but effective way she has co-operated with fellow workers in pushing many another piece of good legislation, but always from the obscurity of the wings rather than before the footlights."

Another of her fans said Peabody always brought "interest and intelligence" to bear upon "all that relates to any questions or matters with which she concerns herself. She is never superficial in anything she undertakes."

Peabody and McClurg made a formidable team.

These two active women represented the new woman of turn-of-the-century America. Providentially, Peabody and McClurg lived in the two communities, Denver and Colorado Springs, that dominated the state in the 1890s. As the product of the 1858-1859 Pike's Peak gold rush, Denver had long been the political, economic, transportation, and financial hub of Colorado, whereas Colorado Springs was initially developed, in the 1870s, by the Denver & Rio Grande Railroad as a health and tourist center. Its mineral springs (really next door in Manitou Springs), Garden of the Gods, Pike's Peak, and other attractions drew people, particularly some well-to-do Englishmen who had invested in the railroad or came because of the western setting. These men and their families turned Colorado Springs into a social and cultural rival of Denver. Denver benefited from Leadville's silver bonanza in the 1870s and 1880s, and Colorado Springs came of age in the 1890s, with Cripple Creek's gold in its back yard.

The two towns emerged as Colorado's leading social and cultural centers and attracted most of the state's socially prominent elite and wealthy families. They provided the perfect basis for gathering women to join the cause, women who had money and time to contribute and were willing and able to work outside the home. At the same time, a danger quietly lurked under the surface. The communities were rivals over a variety of matters. One needed to tread carefully not to arouse civic passions.

Both women became known as "the Mother of Mesa Verde National Park," a conflicting claim if there ever was one. Both of these talented, motivated activists and atypical Victorian women worked passionately to fulfill their dream of saving Mesa Verde. Their story is one of accomplishment, success, and later, personal anguish that led to a cloud that nearly obscured their achievements.

The story of McClurg, Peabody, and their colleagues has much to say about the role of women in turn-of-the-century America. They and others faced an uphill struggle to convince men of their abilities and to break out of the mold in which women had been confined for centuries. They were not alone. Women were actively involving themselves in a fascinating variety of arenas, from suffrage to athletics.

As Eleanor Roosevelt stated a generation later: "I gain strength, courage and confidence by every experience in which I must stop and look fear in the face . . . . I say to myself, I've lived through this and can take the next thing that comes along. We must do the things we think we cannot do." The women of Mesa Verde did that and helped pave the way for those who came after them.

I

WOMEN
ARISE

L ong before McClurg and Peabody had become engrossed in preserving Mesa Verde, women had been interested in projects beyond the home. Men and many women had long presumed that women's role was that of wife and mother. The Victorian stereotype of the husband protecting the "helpless" wife from the outside world predominated. Custom and law made the wife dependent on her husband.

A tiny minority disagreed. Energized and talented, these women came out from under the shadow of their husbands and social expectations. Decades before Queen Victoria took the throne and gave her name to an era, Abigail Adams, for example, had suggested to her husband John that the founding fathers remember women when devising the new government. That suggestion came to naught.

"THE FEW WOMEN WHO DID BECOME INVOLVED IN THE STRUGGLE CAME FROM THE SLOWLY GROWING MIDDLE CLASS, THOSE WHO COULD AFFORD SERVANTS. THEY HAD THE TIME AND ENERGY TO BECOME INVOLVED."

As the nineteenth century opened, women found themselves without the vote, with no role in party politics, and with little place in government. Worldly affairs were not within their realm either. Yet as the reform movement got under way in the 1830s, women were actively involved virtually everywhere. Officially, men might be the leaders, but women provided the backbone, especially in trying to establish temperance, and then prohibition, across the land. They also elicited support for social issues, abolished social "evils" (for instance, fighting prostitution), improved insane asylums, brought about prison reform, and encouraged the establishment of orphanages and hospitals. Some even went as far as forming all-female chapters of organizations to define and achieve their programs.

All of this did not happen without social disapproval. When women became involved in the antislavery movement in Massachusetts, men and even other women criticized them for moving beyond their accepted role. A group of ministers circulated a letter, citing the Bible as their guide, describing the proper role of women and reprimanding them for stepping out of "woman's proper sphere" of silence and subordination. One of the women, Sarah Grimke, wrote a stinging rebuttal: "Men and women were CREATED EQUAL. Whatever is right for a man to do is right for women." Still, women found it a constant struggle to be heard, taken seriously, and granted equality.

The majority of women did not participate in the struggle. They were too busy with housework and raising their children. Families were large in the pre-Civil War era, with four or five children on average. The few women who did become involved in the struggle came from the slowly growing middle class, those who could afford servants. They had the time and energy to become involved.

Women also moved into, and came to dominate, teaching and primary public education. As Caroline Beecher—a member of that famous family—advocated, teaching offered suitable employment for young, single women. Teaching called for nurturing skills and moral values. "Is not woman best fitted to accomplish these important objects?" Beecher asked. They might be, but that did not guarantee equality. Women received half the pay of their male counterparts and found themselves under strict community supervision so they would not stray from virtue's path.

As the 1850s slipped away, one reform—antislavery—came to dominate the scene. Women were involved in that cause, but then came the firing on Fort Sumter, followed by war. The Civil War both sidetracked and helped women. With men marching off to war, "Betsy Yank and Janey Reb" took on new obligations and tasks. For instance, over the objections of some doctors, they became army nurses, and nursing became a new profession for them after the war. Still, during the tense war years the conflict pushed other reforms into the background.

In the postwar years, when McClurg and Peabody reached maturity, more women renewed their push for prewar reform issues, including suffrage, along with that old favorite, prohibition. Starting in 1848, with the Seneca Falls Convention, women's rights conventions were held. One of their leaders, Elizabeth Cady Stanton, stated that "government based on caste and class privilege cannot stand." The women gathered, talked, wrote, and lobbied, and they did make some gains in getting more favorable property and divorce laws passed. Their largest organization, the Woman's Christian Temperance Union, continued its decades-old fight. Jane Addams opened Hull House in Chicago in a slum neighborhood and set standards for help and care that have lasted to this day. She and others also worked for peace. Women, in addition, did some things previously unimaginable, like joining the Knights of Labor, the Grange, and the Farmers' Alliance—each of which supported suffrage and other women's reforms. They had become politically active.

Some women became noted speakers and lecturers as well as organizers. Mary Lease gained national fame when she told farmers to raise "less corn and more hell." She vividly justified the cause: "Ours is a grand, a holy mission, to drive from our land and forever abolish the triune monopoly of land, money, and transportation." The well-known suffragist, Susan B. Anthony, put everything in perspective saying that the country needed to give "men, their rights and nothing more; women, their rights and nothing less."

The response to all this proved tantalizingly slow, but some progress could be seen. Wyoming was the first territorial legislature to give women the right to vote (1869), followed by Utah (1870). In 1893, Colorado men voted to give women the vote in that state, a first by public election. Carrie Catt can take credit for that development and for solidifying the national movement to victory a quarter of a century later. Idaho followed Colorado in 1896.

Not everything had such positive results, however. Women won the vote in Washington in 1883 and lost it four years later in a court decision. Utah women also lost the vote temporarily as part of an attack on polygamy.

Why did these victories occur in the West? Many reasons could be advanced: Women played a major role in western settlement, the region was more egalitarian than the East, the scarcity of women gave them openings their eastern sisters lacked, and the radicalism of western political parties provided them with a forum. Nevertheless, none of these answers is conclusive. A combination of many factors probably resulted in the women's success in each individual state and territory. Whatever the reasons, by 1900 only western states had accepted woman suffrage *in toto*.

On another front, women writers made strides. Though sometimes using pseudonyms, women writers and poets had long been on the American literary scene. Before the Civil War, Harriet Beecher Stowe made a major impact with her *Uncle Tom's Cabin*, and Emily Dickinson eventually had a more quiet effect on U.S. literature. After the war Sarah Jewett, Kate Chopin, and Mary Freeman sometimes shocked their Victorian readers—and sometimes romanticized the world about which they wrote.

The Chautauqua movement sweeping the country involved women as teachers and lecturers as well as students and listeners. Few communities midsized or larger did not have a Chautauqua season at least a week or two in length. Women were even breaking into the hallowed halls of ivy, teaching in higher education. Then came the typewriter, which, according to contemporary comments, fit women's smaller fingers better than men's, and thus they entered the business world in increasing numbers.

Other women blazed new trails. Women now rode bicycles, making them "unfit" to be wives and mothers, some men groused. Some younger women wanted to play the new game of basketball. That would certainly arouse young men's passions, parents complained to school boards. Others joined "bloomer girls" baseball teams and confronted men's teams while young men watched! Hussies all! What was America coming to? Some women even cavorted on beaches in what were declared to be "scanty" outfits that displayed their ankles! The fastidious advocated separate beaches for each sex.

McClurg and Peabody entered this world with their ideas about saving Mesa Verde. They had on their side a further example of women's involvement in the field, one that directly related to what they proposed to do in Colorado: the saving and preservation of George Washington's home at Mount Vernon.

In the 1850s a shy, determined southerner named Ann Pamela Cunningham had founded the Mount Vernon Ladies' Association to save Washington's Potomac River home. Cunningham thereby gave birth to the historical preservation movement in America. At first she simply appealed to "the Ladies of the South," then she implored Northern women to preserve the "Father of the country's" home. In 1858, Cunningham, wanting to avoid sectionalism, turned the association into a national organization and added "of the Union" to the title. She quickly organized committees in various states to promote the effort and raise funds. Under Cunningham's guidance, her cause energized women and became a rousing success. By 1859, association members represented thirty states. With perseverance and courage, the women overcame discouragement and in 1859 succeeded in purchasing the plantation buildings and grounds. They started restoration immediately. The Civil War intervened before they could accomplish much, but the women had saved Mount Vernon for posterity.

Not only did these determined women offer an excellent example to follow, but the Mesa Verde women needed to consider some of their problems, too. Raising money proved a continual problem. The threat of vandalism, the continual need for restoration, and the task of gathering "domestic objects" associated with the lives of Martha and George Washington occupied their attention. Cunningham retired in 1873, leaving behind a commission. She offered this challenge: "Ladies, the home of Washington is in your charge. See to it that you keep it the home of Washington! Let no irreverent hand change it; no vandal hands desecrate [it] with the fingers of—progress!"

Virginia McClurg could have written the same letter, substituting Mesa Verde for Mount Vernon. No doubt, the women of Mount Vernon inspired the women of Mesa Verde. Furthermore, they provided a wonderful example of how women could organize to save, maintain, and preserve a national treasure and, at the same time, keep it open to visitors. By the time of the 1876 Centennial celebration, when visitors were just discovering the fascination of the prehistoric Southwest, Mount Vernon had become a "must see" for those interested in American history.

2

WOMEN
TO THE RESCUE

Balcony House photographed by Gustaf Nordenskiold in 1891.

W ith the sterling model of Mount Vernon, McClurg, and eventually Peabody and other women, set out to save the fascinating ruins that encompassed Mesa Verde. They arrived on the scene none too soon. Locals and others already had their eye on the possibilities of profit from selling relics or at the very least from collecting items to be sent out of the region.

Interest in southwestern antiquities predated McClurg's arrival by generations, dating back to the Spanish arrival in southwestern Colorado in the mid-eighteenth century. The famous Dominguez-Escalante expedition of 1776 reported finding ruins along the Dolores River, after passing by Mesa Verde. The American trader William Becknell, "the Father of the Santa Fe Trail," who had opened the trail and trade with New Mexico, turned to trapping in the winter of 1824-1825. His winter quarters probably lay within the boundaries of the present park, and when trapping proved poor, he had plenty of time to look around. He found an "abundance of broken pottery . . . well baked and neatly painted and many small stone houses, some one story beneath the surface of the earth." His letter gave readers of the *Missouri Intelligence* their first description of the ruins.

This land would be Mexican Territory until 1848, when it became part of the United States following the Mexican-American War. With little thought, the government presented the land to the Utes, who had been residing there for centuries. Settlement seemed far away, and no valuable minerals had been found among the plateaus, mesas, and deserts, so there seemed little reason for concern.

Whether anyone, up to this time, ventured into the canyons and table-lands that constituted Mesa Verde remains unknown. Realistically, one may assume some New Mexicans might have done so, but they failed to leave a record of their adventure. The area acquired Spanish names, which showed those people had passed that way and paused to label what they saw. Uncertainty about visitors soon ended. On August 8, 1859, an adventure-some geologist, Dr. John S. Newberry, a member of the San Juan exploring expedition, climbed the mesa's north side. While admiring the breathtak-ing view, he still felt compelled to write, "To us, however, as well as to all the civilized world, it was a *terra incognita*." Finding nothing to interest him further, and without venturing into the canyons, Newberry climbed back down and rejoined the expedition that skirted Mesa Verde to the north.

The Civil War not only kept Newberry's report unpublished for another decade, but it also gave Mesa Verde its last moments of isolated tranquility. The 1859 Pike's Peak rush brought prospectors to the future Colorado. Within a year they arrived in the nearby Animas Valley and found their way north to their goal—the mountainous San Juans. A mini-rush the fol-lowing year fizzled after they found little gold, faced numbing isolation and elevations, worried about Ute unhappiness with the trespassers (which the prospectors did not think they were), and confronted the 1861 out-break of the war back in the states. Because of the mining rushes, however, Colorado became a territory, and Mesa Verde fell into its domain, although few noticed or cared about an isolated southwest corner. Meanwhile, war swept over the land, and Colorado languished.

The same bewitching lure of gold and silver that had beckoned the Spanish a century before intrigued the Americans as well. By 1869, prospectors had journeyed up the Dolores River north of Mesa Verde, prospecting their rumors, legends, and hopes. The next year they once again ventured into the heart of the San Juans. Although these arrivals were seasonal at first, coming during the warm, relatively snowless months, they heralded permanent settlement and mining.

In 1873 a fascinating, enigmatic, charming New Englander, John Moss, led a prospecting party into La Plata Canyon—which brought permanent settlement there—and along the Mancos River. Moss and his men explored, ranched, and mined for several years without a great deal of monetary success. They did, however, find ruins in Mancos Canyon on the south side of Mesa Verde.

A chance meeting between Tom Cooper (of the Moss party) and his old friend from Omaha, photographer William Henry Jackson, in August 1874 led directly to increased interest in the ruins of the "Aztecs." And the arrival of McClurg, the discoveries by the Wetherill family, and Gustaf Nordenskiold's visit to Mesa Verde would soon follow, meaning the dawn of public interest was at hand.

Two prospectors are packed and ready to go in this 1880s photo taken in Parrott City, near the mouth of La Plata Canyon. Hardly a trace remains of this mining town that was once the La Plata County seat.

Jackson, who had been in the West since 1866 and been a part of the famous Hayden Surveys, had become an enthusiastic, born-again Westerner. His striking photographs of the Yellowstone region had helped persuade Congress to create the nation's first national park. In 1874 Jackson climbed peaks in the towering San Juans, taking photographs as part of the survey. The first view the public saw might have given some prospective San Juaners a start when they comprehended the ruggedness of the region.

Fascinated by the stories of ruins, Jackson and reporter Ernest Ingersoll traveled down to Moss's camp at Parrott City and gladly accepted Moss's offer to guide them to the site of the ruins in Mancos Canyon. On September 9, 1874, toward the end of a long day's journey, Jackson saw his first ruins after feeling a little discouraged because he had found nothing that "really

PARROTT CITY

Mining opened the south-western corner of Colorado as it had the entire state. La Plata Canyon provided one of the earliest excitements in the 1870s, with Parrott City as its principal camp. Designated the county seat of La Plata County in 1876, the camp at best never had more than a couple of hundred people in and about it. Production, meanwhile, by no means matched expectations. With the arrival of Durango on the scene in 1880, and its quickly voting itself the county seat, Parrott City rapidly declined.

Animas Museum Photo Archive

This cabinet card image of John Moss, originally taken by Pueblo photographer Erie, apparently was copied by Durango photographer Jacob A. Boston.

came up to my idea of grand or picturesque for photos." He found his hoped-for site at what later became known as Two Story House. After he had explored and photographed that ruin, Moss took Jackson farther down Mancos Canyon and west to McElmo Canyon. Jackson found a great deal to photograph, but because this was a "hasty trip" he did not venture into Mesa Verde. Nonetheless, he provided the key that opened public interest in the region.

Jackson's photographs and Ingersoll's writings stirred new interest in the "marvelous cities of the cliffs" in southwestern Colorado. Other visitors soon appeared, at first not in a rush, only in a trickle. With the nation's one-hundredth birthday approaching, Jackson again helped promote the region. He helped create models of southwestern archaeological sites for the Centennial Exposition in Philadelphia. Although it was not of the Mesa Verde region, the exhibition, with Jackson there to answer questions, whetted the public's appetite. The display "drew almost as many visitors as Dr. Alexander Graham Bell's improbable telephone." Combined with the writings and relics, the exhibition sparked the beginning of a national archaeological interest in the Southwest, as well as in the still isolated southwestern portion of Colorado, with its "mysterious burial places" and prehistoric ruins.

When the railroad finally arrived in the new town of Durango in 1881, the region's isolation diminished, and the pace of settlement quickened. Even closer to Mesa Verde was the farming and ranching settlement of Mancos, where Moss once had wintered his stock. Only a day's travel from Durango, Mancos sat astride the Mancos River and near Mancos Canyon, the southern doorstep to Mesa Verde. All that was needed now to stimulate interest in the ruins was for some folks to venture into that "thick-matted jungle of undergrowth, tall, reedy grass, willows and thorny bushes, all interlaced and entwined by tough and wiry grape-vines," as Jackson had described the side canyons heading into the heart of the mesa.

In the 1880s a slow trickle of people started arriving to see the ancient ruins of the Aztecs. Realizing that the neighboring Utes had no history of cliff or mesa-top villages and had not lived in anything resembling them, it seemed obvious to nearly everyone that some other group had built the

Gustaf Nordenskiold / Mesa Verde National Park

Wetherill Ranch, Alamo, the starting point for Mesa Verde adventures, photographed by Gustaf Nordenskiold.

dwellings. The best possibility, or so it appeared at the time, was that the advanced and powerful Aztecs of central Mexico must have reached the region. Who else could it have been? It would be several decades before that idea died.

Two of the visitors finally struggled up one of the side canyons into Mesa Verde. S. E. Osburn wrote an article for Denver's *Weekly Tribune Republican* (December 23, 1886) describing how he and Walter Hayes had passed "many pleasant days . . . among the ruins." They also carved their names on a cliff dwelling, thereby establishing a tradition that continued for decades.

The final piece of the puzzle that led to the public discovery of the Mesa Verde ruins came from the Wetherill family, who settled southwest of tiny Mancos. This Quaker family farmed and ran cattle and got along well with their neighbors, the Utes, who in turn allowed them to winter their stock in Mancos Canyon. The Wetherill brothers, Richard, Win, Clayton, Al and John, with time on their hands in their winter camp, started to explore the side canyons.

By 1887 they had visited Balcony House, and Al had seen Cliff Palace but had not visited it. They had also gathered a small collection of relics that they sent to Denver. Their hobby turned into something more when tourists started arriving at their ranch during the pleasant summer and fall months. The tourists wanted to tour some of the ruins and were willing to

Gustaf Nordenskiold / Mesa Verde National Park

Richard, at left and John Wetherill in Mancos Canyon, 1891.

pay for guides. They went through Mancos Canyon and up side canyons, saw a site or two, dug up or collected some souvenirs, and returned to the ranch.

Like other pioneering settlers, the Wetherills sought extra sources of income and they had found them. They could make money from the "Aztec" ruins, and what if a souvenir or two, or even quite a few, left with the visitors? One could always find more where those came from. The turning point came in December 1888, when Richard and his brother-in-law, Charlie Mason, while searching for stray cattle, saw Cliff Palace. Charlie never forgot the experience: "From the rim of the canon we had our first view of Cliff Palace. To me this is the grandest view of all among the ancient ruins of the Southwest." They climbed down, explored, collected some objects, and hurried back to camp.

Over the next thirty days Richard, Charlie, and Richard's brothers John, Clayton, and Al gathered a "fine" collection that they took back to their Alamo Ranch. Father Ben Wetherill, with great foresight, wrote the Smithsonian Institution about buying the collection. Unfortunately, with museum funds short, the Smithsonian became the first, but not the last organization to pass up a momentous opportunity.

The Wetherills, in their own quiet way, realized they had stumbled onto something very significant. They looked beyond mere collecting to preservation of the sites and joined the vanguard, with others who were trying to do the same. In 1889, as the Wetherills explored and exhibited, an archaeological site had already been set aside. It was Arizona's Casa Grande, designated a national monument. On a larger scale, as mentioned, the government had established a national park—Yellowstone—and a few Americans were pushing for the creation of national forests. Concern for conservation and preservation was gaining momentum, both among the public and in the press.

The Wetherills took their collection to Durango in March, where they were amazed by the lively interest it generated. "We had not expected that other people would be as much interested in the collection as we had been," Mason later wrote. They also discovered that people would pay to see the exhibit, a momentous turning point. However, Durango did not have the money to buy their relics, so they traveled to Pueblo. Locals there showed little interest and on they went to the capital city. Denver proved a winner. The Wetherills finally sold the collection, and it found a home; it became the foundation of the Colorado Historical Society's prehistoric collection. The $3,000 price gave the family a nice profit and lighted excitement throughout their Mancos neighborhood.

"WE HAD NOT EXPECTED THAT OTHER PEOPLE WOULD BE AS INTERESTED IN THE COLLECTION AS WE HAD BEEN."

Suddenly, what had been only a curiosity, now had dollar signs attached. For farmers and ranchers who were barely surviving, such a sale represented an unexpected financial windfall unequaled by anything their labor might provide. For them, it looked like a gold strike. The rush was on. Quiet would never again reign in Mesa Verde.

The Wetherills' discovery also publicized the ruins and the area just at the time the Rio Grande Southern Railroad reached Mancos on its way around the western edge of the San Juans. Now tourists could board a train in Denver, ride to Durango, change trains, and depart for Mancos. Arriving in ease and comfort, they then traveled a short distance to the Alamo Ranch where the now famous Wetherills greeted their guests. From there, it was only a day's ride to the heart of Mesa Verde.

As news of the discovery spread, it attracted the attention of a slender, twenty-two-year-old Swedish scholar, Gustaf Nordenskiold, who was traveling in the southern United States in 1891, trying to find relief from his tuberculosis. After touring several southern states, he arrived in Denver, no doubt because he had heard about the wonderful discoveries of ruins of

Welcome to the Cliff Dwellings in Chicago.

Duane A. Smith

ancient peoples. Nordenskiold rode by train to Mancos and finally to the Alamo Ranch, where the Wetherills joined him for an expedition in Mesa Verde that lasted several months.

The outcome of this visit was the publication of Nordenskiold's monumental book, *The Cliff Dwellers of the Mesa Verde*, the initial scholarly examination of the area. His expedition, the first conscientious attempt to systematically excavate and record Mesa Verde archaeology, proved a milestone in American archaeology. Nordenskiold's attempt, though, to take a small collection back to Sweden aroused Durangoans. How dare he take these "American" relics out of the country? They stopped him temporarily, but no law existed under which they could prevent this foreigner from stealing their treasures.

Scholarship proved fine for the academic community. However, for the general public the exhibit at the Columbian Exhibition in Chicago in 1893 stirred greater interest. The mysterious, enchanting "Streets in Cairo," not to mention belly dancers and Buffalo Bill's Wild West Show might have garnered more attention. Nevertheless, for those who could tear themselves away from such treats, "The Cliff-Dwellers" exhibit could be found at the southeast corner of the exhibition grounds. The exhibit was one of the few to charge admission; it cost twenty-five cents to see the wonders and another ten cents for a catalogue.

The fair's guide, *A Week at the Fair*, with misstatements, whetted visitors' interest. A drawing of Cliff Palace graced the description to entice fair-goers to view the dwellings of America's ancient peoples. Americans no longer had to feel inferior to the Old World with its long history. We had our own!

> [Here] is fitly and faithfully reproduced the most ancient civilization of the American Continent. One enters a cavernous portal to find a representation (on a scale of one-tenth the actual size) of the wondrous and long-deserted cliff-dwellings of the Mancos Canon, Colorado. Here in Colorado he [early man] and many of his kind lived, builded with rare art, hunted and tilled the Mesa Verde many thousand years before the pyramids were raised, ages before the Norseman sailed, or the Genoese navigator conceived the idea of a voyage to the West. With an excellent exactitude the H. Jay Smith Exploring Co. have reproduced the finest of the cliff-dwellings, constructed rocky trails for the adventurous to traverse, and arranged a valuable collection of cliff relics for the inspection of the scientist, student, or curious.

The now beguiled fair-goer could explore further. A museum at the end of the canyon included mummies placed "so as not to offend those who did not care to look at such things." It is hoped that they offended few. Without question, they interested many, and it all called attention to southwestern Colorado.

Twelve million or so fair-goers toured the exposition. How many visited the cliff dwellings is unknown, but the publicity and promotion proved priceless. To further add to the lure, the Colorado state exhibit also included a smaller collection of Mesa Verde material, so fair visitors could speculate and wonder about this lost civilization. Although valuable, the publicity was also a threat, because it attracted the curious and a few who hoped to find enough relics to sell. Tourists who were climbing around, poking and prying, gathering souvenirs, and generally not worrying about potential damage to the ruins unintentionally threatened the wonderful heritage they were viewing. More relics wandered off to places unknown.

Also, locals continued busily gathering collections, at best to be sent to museums throughout the country so that they would preserve them. Others came for a day or two to add to personal collections or to find something to sell. Rifling through the ruins and selling a variety of materials became a money-making proposition. The press called them "Sunday diggers," and they came with picks and shovels to see what they could find. Famed archaeologist Earl Morris's father was in Durango in 1891, buying supplies and discussing what he planned to do during the winter. A man overheard him say he intended to do some digging and stated, "I would like to have the first chance to purchase any relics that you find this winter." By the spring of 1892, Morris's father had exhumed quite a collection that he sold to the man, whose name was Gilbert McClurg. Collecting continued throughout the decade.

These were dark days for Mesa Verde, although it was understandable why locals carried on such activities. In the trying times of the 1890s depression, one of the worst in American history, they tried anything that might bring some money their way. The visitors did not realize they were damaging or destroying archaeological material, or that in taking it away from its original location, they were destroying much of its significance. Despite the motive, the result remained the same—the destruction of irretrievable archaeological evidence or, at the least, unintentional damage to sites.

Into this varied world staunchly marched Virginia McClurg, Lucy Peabody, and their friends. They set to work, determined to save and preserve Mesa Verde. They had allies elsewhere, but selling their ideas locally would not be easy for the women when they threatened the economic windfall. The women faced a further challenge. The larger public, as yet, had not caught on to what was occurring at Mesa Verde, or that its amazing heritage was disappearing piece by piece.

More than the heritage was disappearing. Visitors, without much of a second thought, littered in and around the ruins, creating an unsightly mess. All of this concerned people who advocated saving Mesa Verde before it became too late. A few private individuals, as well as people within the federal government, protested against the looting and vandalism. They met a wall of public indifference.

In addition, individuals were not united regarding what should or could be done. Even before Mesa Verde appeared on the scene, people had been worried about other ruins found in the Southwest. They had sent a petition to Congress back in 1882 to preserve "at least some of the extinct cities or puebloes." After a brief discussion, the issue had been laid to rest in a senate committee, from whence it never reappeared. The issue attracted little attention or voter appeal.

As soon as Mesa Verde was discovered, the suggestion was made in 1889 to convert Cliff Palace into "a museum ... filled with relics of the lost people." Others advocated turning it into a state or national park. The Colorado Historical Society, for example, in its 1889-1890 report, recommended that the Colorado General Assembly take action so the area around Mancos Canyon containing the prehistoric ruins would be "set apart for a State or National Park." Nothing came of that suggestion either.

The public and elected representatives needed time to digest and to discuss the issue. Meanwhile, individuals and private groups petitioned Washington, as did the Colorado legislature, all to no avail. The movement needed a determined leader to organize, motivate, and educate people, and to defiantly stay the course. No one else need apply except a person willing to push ahead in the face of certain hostility from some locals, general adversity, and public indifference. This, after all, was a crusade to preserve and ensure that the heritage and significance of Mesa Verde would never be lost.

The Great Divide

Virginia Donaghe McClurg ca. 1888

One visitor complained in the 1890s, "Although these ruins are presumably the property of the National Government, little, if anything, has been done to preserve them." Author F. H. Newell of the United States Geological Survey, writing in *National Geographic* (October 1898), put his finger on an even better source of potential monetary return than pot hunting. "It is a matter of regret that these interesting ruins are not being preserved as even from a commercial aspect they would have an ever increasing value to that part of the state in attracting tourists from all over the world."

Where was the savior? Fortunately, such a person, in true western fashion, rode to the rescue—the irrepressible Virginia Donaghe, soon to be McClurg. She launched an emotional one-woman campaign—initially in Colorado and then in the rest of the United States—to save the ruins and establish a park. Her interest dated from the early 1880s.

Virginia McClurg first visited the cliff dwellings at Mesa Verde in 1886. Despite claiming to be the first to visit Balcony House, she was not; yet the visit sparked her interest in the ruins, and she took her first tentative steps toward preservation. Out of this came a series of sketches, "Cliff Climbing in Colorado," that appeared in Colorado Springs newspapers. More articles appeared in the *Great Divide* during its initial year in 1889.

Her fictionalized, romanticized account, mentioned earlier, ran through several issues and was based on her own visit. McClurg's description of Durango (March 1889) provides a classic sample of her writing style.

Durango, La Plata county, our outfitting point, is, as one of its pioneers has left on record with charming candor, "the most *un*relicky place on the globe." Notwithstanding its modern tendencies and western iconoclasm, to say nothing of its dependence upon and deference to its big smelter, even Durango (built like Resina over Herculaneum) contains within its boundaries two ruined estufas, marked by circular mounds and occupies the land where an earlier race probably reared its tenements.

"The Enthusiast" (McClurg) claims to have previously been to the ruins in 1885 and serves, as mentioned, as narrator of the group's adventures.

The articles are more than simply an adventurous travelogue; drawings are included to create even more of an exciting atmosphere. Virginia Donaghe had done her homework, and she brought the reader up to date on earlier articles about the cliff people. She also discussed theories of who these people might have been. She covered the gamut from the "Ten Lost Tribes of Israel" to survivors from Atlantis to the Chinese, Greeks, and Mongols. To her, the cliff dwellers were likely the Aztecs or some other group from central Mexico.

The articles and the news of the Wetherills' discovery came out nearly simultaneously. Mesa Verde was becoming better known almost by the month.

Following her marriage and after the birth of her son, McClurg had even more time to develop her interests and talents. Her first venture into making the public aware of Mesa Verde came in 1892, when she gave a "course"—really a series of stereopticon lectures—in Denver on "house-building aborigines of our southwest." At the close of this series, a petition "asking for the preservation of prehistoric ruins" was drawn up and circulated. From this came the "first glimmerings," as McClurg described it, of an organized movement to save the ruins.

Her efforts came to a halt for three years after that, when she went East. But upon returning she jumped full force into an organized effort. McClurg came back a determined, dedicated woman. With a resolve that would brook no compromise she set forth on her crusade. Unfortunately, she planted the seeds of trouble, the harvest of which awaited the future. For the moment, she needed to educate and arouse the public to the threat she saw to her beloved Mesa Verde.

As a start, she addressed women's clubs and, then, in Pueblo in 1897, she spoke at the state meeting of the Federation of Women's Clubs. The group organized a committee for the "restoration and preservation of the cliff dwellings and pueblo ruins in Colorado," and McClurg emerged as the logical choice for chairperson.

The timing proved perfect. The late nineteenth century saw a proliferation of women's associations, which grew at an energetic pace and tackled a range of issues and problems. These associations allowed thousands "of conventional middle-class women" to learn from others, become involved in civic affairs, and work toward common goals. Homebound matrons mingled with like minded "sisters," shared their interests and gained confidence and experience in a variety of ways and with many causes. The vitality of these movements generated momentum, and the members' enthusiasm swept vigorously across the country and into Colorado.

Typically, these middle- and upper-class women met for weekly meetings that featured lectures, discussions, and book reports. They raised funds to support worthy projects and discussed ways to advance their "causes." Being typical Americans, they organized into local, state, and national organizations. Virginia McClurg could not have asked for a better forum or a more enthusiastic audience.

She gave speeches and illustrated lectures (using glass slides plus a gas lantern projector) and organized and wrote articles, including "The Cliffs and Pueblos of Colorado." She lobbied, writing Colorado senators Henry Teller and Edward Wolcott, about saving the ruins and seeking information, particularly if the ruins resided on Ute land. She did not "dread the presence of the Utes," but McClurg wanted to protect the sites from the "miners, cowboys and relic-hunters." The federal government seemed her best hope.

"CLIFF PALACE IS THE PREY OF THE SPOILER; SOON IT WILL BE TOO LATE TO GUARD THESE MONUMENTS."

Teller initially opposed setting aside the cliff dwellings as a national park. The June 13, 1899, *Denver Times*, supported by the *Mancos Times*, promptly took him to task, saying there "is not one foot of ground . . . that can be made available for agricultural purposes." The papers pointed out further that "some steps should certainly be taken to preserve these remarkable reminders of an ancient population." Teller pondered the women's request and awaited other developments.

Meanwhile, in a speech at a Colorado Women's Club meeting (October 1898), McClurg laid out her plans. She wanted to keep the subject "fresh in the public mind," gain for the women the custodianship of Mesa Verde, and continue working on "national preservation." McClurg warned her listeners, "Cliff Palace is the prey of the spoiler; soon it will be too late to guard these monuments."

Thus, Mesa Verde's Paul Revere galloped about, arousing the public and gathering recruits. Well into a crusade that would occupy her for the rest of her life, McClurg possessed a born-again Christian's excited fervor.

McClurg had reached nearly the halfway point in her Mesa Verde campaign, although she had no way to know that. She sensed the urgency, the need, and she must have sensed that her appeal was touching other women. The way ahead looked long, perhaps troubling; however, that did

Durango, railroad and tourist hub for Mesa Verde.

not seem to worry her. The popular English novelist and poet of the day, Rudyard Kipling, offered this advice:

> If you can meet with Triumph and Disaster
> And treat those two impostors just the same.
> If you can talk with crowds and keep your virtue,
> Or walk with Kings—nor lose the common touch.
> Yours is the Earth and everything that's in it.

McClurg would meet and experience all these things in the years ahead. Kipling's caution against treating them the same would stand her in good stead, if she had stepped back a moment to take stock of what was occurring around her. That would not be easy, for as the pace picked up in the coming years, McClurg would find herself in the limelight as never before in her life.

3

TRIUMPH
AND TRAGEDY

Everything seemed to be slowly falling into place for Virginia McClurg. With her enthusiasm and never-say-die spirit she continued her educational campaign. The young author's excitement, shown in the *Great Divide* articles, continued unabated. The future seemed unlimited, but she might well have pondered what Shakespeare wrote in *Hamlet*: "Our wills and fates do so contrary run that our devices still are overthrown."

Her heartfelt appeals quickly gathered others to her cause including Lucy Peabody, probably back around 1892. Peabody quickly was able to get a "strong endorsement" from the Bureau of Ethnology for the women's work at Mesa Verde, a valuable endorsement. Most who initially joined with McClurg were Coloradans. Some were rich; others simply gave of their time, talents, and enthusiasm.

"DURANGO'S FEMALE "MOVERS AND SHAKERS" CAME MOSTLY FROM THE READING CLUB OF DURANGO. ...THEY BECAME PILLARS OF THE PRESERVATION MOVEMENT."

Helen Stoiber of Silverton, wife of a prosperous mine owner, entertained members of the 1898 federation meeting in her home at Waldheim, beautifully located just outside the mining town, and she sent a special train to Denver to pick them up. Although Stoiber stayed out of the limelight, she became a pillar in the movement and a staunch friend of McClurg's. Natalie Hammond—wife of the renowned mining engineer John Hays Hammond—became a convert, toured Mesa Verde, brought a photographer along, and took to the lecture circuit with talks on "The Cliff Dwellings of Mesa Verde." She also donated $250 to clean out and enlarge the spring at Spruce Tree House.

Few of McClurg's supporters offered this kind of financial aid. Durangoan Estelle Camp entertained groups on their way to Mesa Verde, and she ventured forth to meet with the Utes in hopes of gaining an agreement concerning the land on which the ruins were situated. She was joined by neighbors Alice Bishop, who led the group that talked to the Utes, and Bishop's mother, Jeanette Scoville, both of whom also entertained visitors. Bankers' wives seemed to have been particularly active, likely having more available time and money to allow them to absorb themselves in such an effort. Besides Camp, Ella McNeil lobbied in Washington, D.C., and Luna Thatcher was actively involved from her home in Pueblo. Denver, Pueblo, Durango, and Colorado Springs society matrons such as Emma Eldredge, Sarah Decker, Sadie Rockwood, and Annie Whitmore also joined the cause.

WOMEN'S WORK

The women who "saved" Mesa Verde
reflected the status of many of their activist
contemporaries. They were typically middle-
or upper class individuals with time, education, enthusiasm, and finances on their side.
In a variety of ways they went beyond the
Victorian stereotype of the role of the wife
and mother in the home and in the church.

Estelle Camp, for example, the wife of
Durango banker Alfred Camp, was very active
in her community. She helped organize the
Durango Reading Club, worked on the City
Improvement Association and Library
Association, served on the Board of Directors
of her husband's bank, and aided in beautify-
ing her community by starting the planting of
trees along the Boulevard, now Third Avenue.
She and others collected Mesa Verde relics to
send with the La Plata County exhibit at the
Columbian Exhibition in Chicago in 1893.

Duane A. Smith

Estelle Camp

Ella McNeil was Estelle Camp's sister. Like her
brother-in-law, McNeil's husband John was an officer in Durango's First National
Bank. She lobbied Congressmen, searched for a lost map in Washington, D.C.,
and was active in a variety of Durango activities regarding the future park.

Alice Bishop's husband was a wealthy inventor who helped develop the elec-
trocardiograph. She proved to be willing to go where few Victorian women
would have ventured and became a "tireless negotiator."

Nicknamed "Captain Jack" by the miners, Helen Stoiber assisted her husband with his mining operations. Newsworthy throughout her life, she was
quite controversial because of her "imperious" and absolutely "fearless manner,"
but she loyally fought to save Mesa Verde. Stoiber could always be counted on
to give a luncheon or reception or donation.

Durango's female "movers and shakers" came mostly from the Reading
Club of Durango. Even before McClurg became actively involved, in 1893
they had collected and sent relics from Mesa Verde to the Chicago's World
Fair to be included in La Plata County's exhibit. Now they became pillars
of the preservation movement.

They were not only actively involved, but they studied their subject.
Estelle Camp entertained the group's February 27, 1903, meeting, for
example, and the minutes reported "a very pleasant" time was had by all.

The Reading Club of Durango worked diligently to save Mesa Verde.

The women "very much enjoyed the exhibit of Indian blankets, baskets and pottery." The speaker discussed "Indian pottery, baskets and the Moqui village." Refreshments concluded "one of the pleasantist meetings of the year." Writing later about the history of the club, the historian—probably Estelle—summarized the club's involvement with Mesa Verde: "In co-operation with women of Denver & Colo. Springs we did much hard work & took some exciting trips in the interest of the Mesa Verde Cliff Dwellings Association."

Virginia McClurg used a variety of approaches trying to stimulate interest including writing to Ada McKinley, the president's wife, about making Mesa Verde a park. McClurg hoped Mrs. McKinley would discuss the issue with her husband. Instead, she received a chilly note from an assistant secretary to the president telling her to take the plea to the secretary of the interior and not bother the president or his wife, who suffered from health problems. A letter to Vice President Theodore Roosevelt received a much more favorable reply, but he did not immediately take up the cause.

Senator Teller seemed a roadblock. His reluctance stemmed from his concern about more federal government encroachment and uneasiness regarding the creation of national forests. Teller and other westerners worried about taking away the rights of nearby settlers and the issue of natural resources. They did not want any potentially mineable resources being "locked up" and therefore unavailable for development. Ella McNeil visited him in Washington, and her appeal must have helped change his mind. He

Cliff Palace looking northeast 1890s.

SAVING MESA VERDE:
A FEMALE CAUSE CÉLÈBRE

Natalie Hammond's popular lecture on "The Cliff Dwellings of Mesa Verde" showed her interest after she visited the ruins in 1900. Like the others, she braved the rugged region with little water and, despite discomforts, came to love Mesa Verde.

Carrie Walsh gained the spotlight when her husband developed the famous Camp Bird Mine nearby the late 1890s. A charter member of the association, she was described by her daughter Evelyn as the "most refined woman" she ever knew. Well educated, with plans to be a teacher, she understood the importance of the Mesa Verde discoveries. The "eloquent" Walsh encouraged her husband to open his "golden treasure box" just in time to be a help to the women's efforts.

All these women also worked hard to raise money in a variety of ways, as well as educate themselves about the "ancient ones."

Colorado women had gotten the vote in 1893; the first state where men had voted to give them that responsibility. Whether or not this encouraged them to go beyond the home cannot be ascertained, but without question their struggle to preserve Mesa Verde was the women's highlight effort in turn-of-the-century Colorado.

did insist, however, that an accurate map of the Mesa Verde area would be "indispensable" to save the ruins.

McClurg, too, visited Washington, and she had an interview with Senator Edward Wolcott. She hoped to gain his support for the federation's application for custodianship of the ruins. She explained her plan was "to act as custodians of specific ruins while the matter of the national preservation process slowly is pending." If the federation gained the custodianship, it would attempt to employ "suitable custodians."

Ever active, McClurg had an idea about who the custodians should be: the Ute police. She traveled to the reservation to talk to the Ute agent about using them, but she knew such a move would not be appreciated: "The employment of such guardians would be an unpopular measure in the Southwest." Yet McClurg believed it would "be both practical and economical should the ruins pass" to the federation's control. She was willing to proceed and thought $10 per month would be a fair wage.

This was part of a larger plan "to continue to keep the subject of Mesa Verde fresh in the public mind." That she did; Mesa Verde was getting better known every year. Few of her other ideas ever came to pass, however. While promising, the future still appeared uncertain, but that did not daunt McClurg.

Although she had a committee to work through, McClurg decided her own organization might be more effective. Some hard feelings existed as the *Denver Republican* (June 24, 1899) pointed out in discussing "recent agitation [unidentified] among prominent members of the Women's clubs of Colorado." As a result, in May 1900 the Colorado Cliff Dwellings Association was incorporated. The names of the incorporators and officers were McClurg, Peabody, Eldredge, Whitmore, Thatcher, Summer, and another Puebloan, Rebecca Lewis.

The new organization seemed particularly important if the women wanted to gain control over the ruins, a plan McClurg advocated more strongly every year. With an initiation fee of $2, annual dues of $1, and a life membership of $100 (life membership being hereditary through the female descendants), the association carried forth its program with McClurg as first regent and Peabody as second regent. The group eventually organized chapters in four other states—California, Utah, Arizona, and New York. Interestingly, California apparently tried to limit membership to "cultured Christian women," when their group organized in 1903. Other states may have organized, but Colorado remained the key player, the bedrock of the movement. It had the leaders and activists and Mesa Verde in its southwest corner.

Men could join with their wives as a team, as did the Hammonds, among others. So did Ouray millionaire Thomas Walsh, husband of member Carrie Walsh. In Colorado, men could join on their own. For example, Al Wetherill was the association representative in Mancos and often guided for the women.

**Women arrived early at Mesa Verde. Jesse Fairfield at base of wall.
Mary Ayers sitting on wall.**

To carry out their ideas and plans, the women had to raise money.
McClurg, in 1901, challenged each member to raise $10. The association
planned a rummage sale that fall, too, and she "kindly" asked members for
"suitable articles." McClurg came up with several ideas about raising money,
including the novel notion to request, "of everyone of her acquaintances" she
happened to see, the "sum of 10 cents." She must have seen quite a few
friends, for she reported "in less than three weeks to have collected $15. . . .
No one minds giving 10 cents, besides it makes the laudable work of the
Association known, and is the best advertisement far and wide."

There had been talk of a state park or a national park at Mesa Verde
from the very start. Virginia McClurg had other ideas and openly stated,
"let this be the women's park." She worried that under federal protection
everything would go to the Smithsonian, and she did not like the idea of a
Colorado state park either. She bluntly asserted that "a state that considers
closing its institutions of learning, and cannot care for her blind, poor, and
insane" held no fascination for her. In an interview, she praised the Chicago
and Hartford, Connecticut, women for their work on various projects,
adding that she knew Mesa Verde would be an even "greater work."

Work, yes, with a little society mixed in as well. The association met once a year for a business meeting plus a social event. They quite often met at McClurg's home in Colorado Springs or at Denver's Brown Palace.

The group focused on two goals: education and practical work. Peabody became chair of the legislative committee. Her Washington experience proved invaluable, so education and lobbying became her forte. For the association's work, a better choice could not have been made. Peabody was a stalwart in the crusade.

The practical work—which was often educational as well—that had been done before now gained momentum. According to the *Mancos Times* in October 1899, the women intended to oversee construction of wagon roads and trails, restore partially caved-in buildings and towers, build stairways to otherwise inaccessible ruins, and excavate for relics to preserve them. With a certain amount of state chauvinism, they wanted to save the relics for Colorado "instead of [giving them] to the Smithsonian Institute." They also planned to "put up a hotel for visitors," who they knew would come. As ambitious as these plans were, they managed to accomplish most of them, although the hotel would never be built.

Residents of Mancos, who had been pushing for a "wagon road to the famous Cliff Dwellings" for several years, held high expectations: "Such a road will cause thousands of dollars to be distributed annually in this village (which will soon be a city) by tourists, and the rest of the county will benefit correspondingly." The *Mancos Times* editor concluded (November 18, 1898), "hundreds of wealthy tourists who visit Colorado Springs would annually visit those wondrous abodes of an extinct race, and Mancos would become the Mecca of the archaeologist." Locals could hardly wait!

Durango, because of its larger size, better accommodations, and its enthusiastic association members became the staging point for expeditions into Mesa Verde, despite Mancos' great hopes. Also, the community's most prestigious women's group, the Reading Club, had long been a force in favor of preserving the ruins. A certain amount of jealousy and rivalry naturally existed between Mancos and Durango, and Durango surging to the forefront regarding Mesa Verde did not help matters. Fortunately, the rivalry did not seriously derail any of the women's efforts.

It did cause some problems, however. Cortez, Mancos, and Durango all proclaimed themselves "gateways" to Mesa Verde and did not want to yield an inch to a rival. This jealousy, according to Mancos folks, caused some "insidious knockers" to try to defeat the women and Mancos. Particularly, they felt that someone had gotten the ear of the Utes in an attempt to defeat any lease agreement.

Durango gained most of the attention as the association moved ahead. For instance, the *Durango Evening Herald* (September 4, 1901) carried this item:

Mrs. Charles Eldredge arrived last evening from Colorado Springs in route to Mancos, where she is to make arrangements for the

Cortez Stage Stables, Mesa Verde Group.

party of scientists who are going to explore the cliff ruins. Mrs. Eldredge states the party consists of about twenty-five, most of whom will be ladies, members of the Cliff Dwellers association for preservation of the ruins, there being six noted scientists. The party leaves Denver this evening, arrives tomorrow afternoon going to Mancos the following morning. While here the members of the reading club will entertain the visitors with a reception and probably show them about the city. Mrs. Eldredge left for Mancos this morning and will attend to securing conveyances for the party. The reception will be held at the residence of Mrs. Thomas Rockwood.

Careful planning went into preparations, they wanted to be sure their guests enjoyed themselves and saw the "wonders" of Durango.

A reception committee of the Reading Club welcomed the guests at the depot. While in town, the women acted as their hosts, enthusiastically showed them around Durango, and held a reception for the distinguished visitors. The group apparently had a good time, as the *Herald* stated the next evening. "A reception was tendered the visitors at the residence of Mrs. Rockwood where a delightful evening was spent evidently being enjoyed by the tourists as they remained until 11 o'clock." The group included Peabody, McClurg, noted archaeologist Jesse Fewkes, and a correspondent for the *New York Herald*. The only negative aspect of the stay was the fact that President William McKinley was shot in Buffalo, New York.

Nine days later, while the party was at Mesa Verde, he died from the wound.

From Durango, the group journeyed on to Mancos. There McClurg proudly took them into "Cliff Canyon" on a wagon road whose development the women had overseen. The women provided guides, equipment, and "commissariat" for their visitors as they toured the ruins. The purpose of the trip was to drum up support for their campaign, and it was only one of several such expeditions. It

Animas Museum Photo Archives

Off to Mesa Verde. Train Depot Durango.

worked. Marie Maule, the *Herald* reporter, wrote an article about her visit and supported the national park bill in Congress. McClurg's reaction remained publicly unrecorded. Others came too, including a six-member party of the Texas Women's Press Club, as the public became more aware of women and their park crusade.

Virginia McClurg also enjoyed playing the role of *grandame* of Mesa Verde. The *Colorado Springs Telegraph* (September 17, 1901) reported:

> The Colorado Cliff dwellings are to be studied and explored by expert authorities with the view of establishing one of two theories as to the origin of the inhabitants, whether they were an off shoot of the southern or Mexican civilization or whether the Mexican civilization was an off shoot of the southwestern. This investigation will be conducted by Senor Leopold Batres, the inspector general of national monuments for Mexico, whom his government has sent out for the purpose.

Señor Batres stopped in Colorado Springs, where McClurg and the association graciously gave him permission to study Mesa Verde to see if he could find any evidence in the ruins.

Batres held the view "that the Mexican civilization was an outgrowth of this [southwest], and will endeavor to establish the fact." The association disagreed. They clearly stated, "the directly opposite view is held by most of the members of the Association." Batres planned to spend three weeks at

LASSOING GOATS.

COLORADO.—IGNATIO, CHIEF OF THE SOUTHERN UTES, ESCORTING THE WOMEN, CHILDREN AND STOCK IN THE ANIMAS VALLEY TO A PLACE OF SAFETY.
FROM A SKETCH BY J. J. REILLY.—SEE PAGE 271.

Center of Southwest Studies/Fort Lewis College

Sketch, by J.J. Reilly, of Chief Ignacio escorting women, children and animals in the Animas Valley. This sketch appeared in *Frank Leslie's Illustrated Newspaper*, June 18, 1881. These are the Utes the women negotiated with about Mesa Verde.

Mesa Verde. No follow-up article appeared to reveal whether he changed his view. Rampant speculation became the order of the day regarding where these ancient people had come from and when they arrived and left.

The women, dealing with a less quixotic idea in a more practical vein, had a survey of the land completed to locate water sources, ruins, and possible road routes. A committee went to Mesa Verde to check out a proposed road, for example. Out of this came the first accurate map of the Mesa Verde area, something Senator Teller had advocated. Realizing the need for a better water source, they improved the spring at Spruce Tree House, now called Hammond Spring after its benefactor. One association member accompanied the surveyors and workers. The women did not let anything escape their attention. A continual concern, though, was the issue of who controlled the land. This led to a fascinating adventure with the Ute Mountain Utes, whose reservation seemingly encompassed the ruins.

McClurg, as mentioned, had been interested in this problem for several years. The federal government had recently divided the Utes into two agencies, giving those who wanted a communal reservation the western part of the old Ute reservation. This included the Mesa Verde ruins, and the women would have to deal with that group which was headed by Ignacio.

Initial efforts in 1897-1898 failed. The Utes appeared disinterested in giving up the ruins. Even if they had, the women had no authority under the law to buy or lease the land. Then a sign of trouble appeared within the committee. It was hinted that personal jealousies and personality clashes handicapped the effort and produced a "lack of unanimity." No further facts emerged, but this might have been the opening salvo of the national park vs. women's park tribulations.

Just after she created her own association, in October 1899, McClurg visited Ignacio and his followers at agency headquarters at Navajo Springs. Her initial intent was to persuade the Utes to consent to establishing a state park before she approached the Department of the Interior.

"After an interesting pow-wow," according to the *Mancos Times,* (October 20), the Utes agreed to a thirty-year lease at a yearly rental of $300, with $300 "up-front money." The Utes had grazing rights within the lease, and the right to appoint special policemen to file complaints "against any person demolishing the ruins or digging" for relics. The women would control the immediate supervision of the state park.

According to the *Times,* Ignacio "created nervousness by suggesting the entire $9,000 be plunked down in one pop." The stunned women had not been ready for that, but the crisis soon passed, and the $9,000 did not have to be paid all at once. For McClurg, this was all wonderful. "Oh, if I could but paint for you the glories of the Mesa Verde in its autumn dress of gold and crimson," she told a reporter.

The Utes agreed to a lease, but only if their agent and the Interior Department agreed. That would take time. Not wanting to wait for the needed approvals, the association sent four Durango women back to Navajo Springs the next year with a "treaty." Association veterans Estelle Camp and Alice Bishop led the group, which traveled by train to Mancos and then on a "hot and dusty ride by horse and buggy." They succeeded in obtaining the signatures of the agent and several Ute "chieftains." Then they received a "special treat" that caused them to fear for their lives. Worried, but too late to return, they stayed the night.

> The ladies were kept awake all night by the shouting and singing as the braves became roaring drunk to celebrate signing the agreement. The agency was not fired as they feared it would be, and the ladies returned to find that still other delays were in store before the final congressional action was completed.

The terrified and utterly proper Victorian women had done something many of their contemporaries would not have considered doing.

One delay was caused by the fact that private citizens had no authority

Early day visitors at Mesa Verde.

to sign such agreements, and, as far as Washington was concerned, a majority of the tribe had not authorized the lease. Undaunted, back they came. The lease agreement was redrawn and submitted the next year, only to be rejected again. The infuriated McClurg exploded: "The department fondly imagines that Weeminuche Utes sit at ease at their agency, pens and blotting paper in hand, ready to sign leases, but such is not the case." As late as 1904, McClurg continued to try to get the Utes to cede the land. A visit to Navajo Springs with United States Senator Thomas Patterson got the association no further. The Utes now refused because they claimed the "government was not treating them fairly" in regard to region, treaty obligations, and irrigation water. Later they added that Senator Patterson seemed to be a "Squaw Man," dominated by "a woman," and thus "they would not deal with him."

Meantime, as the women pushed to save the ruins, tourists appeared in steadily increasing numbers after the turn of the century. The numbers of people were not large because, even with railroad connections, the region remained off the beaten track. Still, the *Mancos Times* (August 24, 1900) reported, "Never before [have] there been so many Cliff Dwellings tourists as at present." Two things had happened—increasing numbers of tourists and increasing souvenir gathering. This made it even more crucial to establish a park before even more relics disappeared or vandalism occurred. The association put up signs along the roads and trails, "prohibiting trespassing and tearing down the masonry of the dwellings and carrying away pottery and implements." Fortunately, now, the association members gained some adherents to the cause from among the visitors. People came, realized the need, and joined the effort.

While all this had been going on, the women under Peabody's guidance had also been active in Washington, where they pushed for a national park. In July 1900, McClurg appeared to shift direction and become "quite confident of ultimate success" in their quest. This change of heart about the future of Mesa Verde seemed perplexing to many people. Perhaps McClurg had been pressured from within her group for Mesa Verde to become a national park as opposed to a woman's park. Opposition to a state park had appeared nationally, and it seems logical that a woman's park might have aroused similar feelings. As one writer expressed it, the task of preserving American antiquities "is too arduous for private individuals." Putting the creation of the park ahead of her own wishes, McClurg pushed ahead, albeit still with reservations.

Peabody supported the national park idea without reservations, and her efforts left "no stone unturned." During the struggle to attain a national park, she "made several trips to Washington at her expense." She lobbied, pigeonholed people, spoke at hearings, and mobilized the support of others. Colorado's congressional delegation tried repeatedly in the early years of the new century to get a bill through Congress. The most supportive was Representative John Shafroth, who warned McClurg in 1900 that the introduction of a bill to create a state park would "raise the most severe opposition" from archaeological societies and the Smithsonian. He supported the national park idea and a House bill to create Colorado Cliff Dwellings National Park. The bill died in committee, as did similar bills in 1902 and 1903—even with McClurg traveling to Washington to testify.

The bills met with opposition from the secretary of the interior because of problems with the Utes and surveys, and because of resistance from cost conscious congressmen, who were not in the least sure a park in a far isolated corner of Colorado would be worth the expense. Who would travel such a distance to see ruins?

Some concern was raised about who would control the right to excavate and collect relics; the Smithsonian Institution hoped for that sole right. Questions also surfaced about homesteaders, who had already taken up land within the potential park boundaries, and about a park cutting off individuals from potentially discovering and developing natural resources. Previously, coal miners had dug near the western end of Mesa Verde to supply the needs of Cortez, which was isolated from the railroad and lacked easy access to coal from outside sources. Locals had high hopes for those deposits.

Westerners did not take kindly to their "rights" being denied or curbed by Uncle Sam. They looked about and saw the national forest movement in full swing and were not pleased, sometimes even to the point of shooting at forest rangers. Now came the federal government under another guise to take away their land and cherished opportunities.

Despite tireless efforts, the women continued to suffer repeated setbacks in Washington. Finally though, they started to gain support. Persistence and education had gained them a toehold. A 1904 attempt to create a park died when the House failed to act, after Colorado senators Henry Teller and Edward Wolcott had guided a bill through to passage in their chamber. With Theodore Roosevelt in the White House, the executive branch was more favorable toward such an idea.

Many signs indicated that the women's efforts might have turned the corner. The government, for example, published a pamphlet about the prehistoric ruins of the Southwest in 1904. It forthrightly emphasized that preservation needed to be pushed with vigor and stated the issue had become a matter of much concern for the American people. More important, the author believed that no barriers hindered the "speedy accomplishment" of turning this awareness into saving the ruins. At home too, the women picked up support in urban areas where people were not so concerned about losing access to potential natural resources.

Nationally, the same change slowly occurred, as indicated by a government pamphlet. Unimaginatively titled "Circular Relating to Historic and Prehistoric Ruins of the Southwest and Their Preservation," the pamphlet praised Mesa Verde as offering the finest specimens of "true cliff dwellings." Such accolades pleased the women, as did the pamphlet's conclusion that a national park established at Mesa Verde would "be of great educational value." The pamphlet suggested the name Colorado Cliff Dwellings National Park. By whatever name, it seemed that the cherished park was marching closer to becoming reality, although it still appeared to lie tantalizingly just beyond the association's reach.

McClurg, Peabody, and others warned that the issue was more urgent than ever. Vandalism and relic removal continued. If anything was to be preserved for the American people to see and for archaeologists to study, action had to be taken now—not promised for tomorrow or sometime in the distant future.

Colorado Senator Thomas Patterson joined with his colleague Henry Teller and the rest of the Colorado delegation in 1905 to push for a national park bill. Representative Herschel Hogg (Shafroth was no longer in the House) shepherded a bill through the House, and Patterson would try to do the same when it reached the Senate. Some association members held reservations about Hogg's bill because it did not, in their opinion, preserve all the sites, and it gave exclusive control over the park to the secretary of the interior, an issue that caused growing uneasiness among the association members. Although the bill gained the support of the Colorado Historical Society and several archaeological societies throughout the country, it died just as its predecessors had.

Group near Spruce Tree House.

When the new congressional session opened in December 1905, Hogg reintroduced a Mesa Verde National Park bill, as did Patterson the next month in the Senate. Finally, the years of lobbying, promoting, and educating paid dividends. From President Roosevelt to his secretary of the interior, through Congress to the people of Colorado, the mood seemed to favor the national park plan.

The national scene benefited the crusade as well. Theodore Roosevelt's presidency energized the Progressive reform era. Reform, in a variety of manifestations, swept over the country, just the thing to boost Mesa Verde. Also, the popular Roosevelt used his office as a "bully pulpit" to advance his favorite subjects, one of the most important of which was conservation. Within this larger movement individuals arose who supported conservation as a way to preserve wilderness for its inherent aesthetic, spiritual, and moral value. The national park movement accommodated those goals beautifully.

Mesa Verde presented the preservation opportunity of a lifetime. It possessed, in its supporters' eyes at least, aesthetic, spiritual, and moral value that was unsurpassed—if not as a wilderness, then as a national historic treasure. The national park would conserve this irreplaceable treasure for posterity and, as a bonus, also would conserve some pristine southwestern canyon and mesa land with its flora and fauna.

Mesa Verde made Mancos famous. Mancos Main Street.

Both Hogg's and Patterson's bills survived the death march through committee and reached their respective floors. Again, pressure was brought to bear on members of Congress. Colorado Governor Jesse McDonald had written earlier: "The People of Colorado, and I believe of the entire West, would be glad to see this bill favorably reported upon by your committee [Senate], as we are quite anxious that this historical place be properly protected." Various groups also sent petitions and letters in support.

Testimony from "professors, learned people and other prominent people" in support of the bill called attention to the national significance of the ruins and the destruction that had already occurred. Did the land have other uses? No, they answered, agriculture had little opportunity here and neither did ranching, because the land was classified as "poor range at best." Further, no profitable deposits of minerals and fuel resources existed within the park boundaries, although there were small coal veins to the west. The potential tourist market offered intriguing potential, with proponents claiming a park "would bring money into such towns as Durango and Mancos." This, in turn, would benefit everybody in the neighborhood. Railroad companies and others argued that a properly developed park would be a tourist Mecca. A downpour of dollars loomed.

Edgar Hewett, long associated with the women and the movement, carefully explained the reasons why the park had to be created and now, not later: "These are unquestionably the greatest prehistoric monuments within the limits of the United States. Aside from their great historic and scientific value," he felt no other cultural or natural wonders "would be of more general interest to the public." Hewett added that "irrepressible damage" had already been done and was "being done," and in addition the "deterioration progresses very rapidly."

The Mesa Verde park bill was not the only one being considered. An equally long-overdue idea gained momentum. A second major bill gained congressional consideration: an antiquities bill that would preserve historic and prehistoric ruins and monuments on government lands. Hewett "worked assiduously" for this legislation as well. Earlier efforts to get the bill passed died, but now it lived again. Public awareness and support came from all areas of the country for this bill as well.

The combination of these factors seemed to point to success as the bills moved slowly toward final approval. Then a stumbling block appeared in Mesa Verde's path. Again, Hewett explained the consequences. He warned that the great cliff houses—Spruce Tree, Balcony, and Cliff Palace—still seemed to lie within the Ute reservation, if the map accompanying the bills proved accurate. The bill being considered, therefore, provided inadequate protection for the "greatest ruins." Hewett recommended the simple expedient of extending the jurisdiction of the park five miles to "encompass that desired end." Doing so

MISS COLORADO: "THEY'LL BE SAFER IN YOUR CARE, UNCLE!"

Victory is celebrated.

would not be an injustice to the Utes, since both "they and the land are under the jurisdiction of the Department of the Interior."

The association supported Hewett, as its members had been concerned about the sites' location. Part of the problem had always been the difficulty of surveying in the intermixed canyons stretching around Mesa Verde. After another survey had been conducted to determine with certainty where the "notable cliff ruins as designated by Prof. Hewett" were found, his amendment was added. The amended bills passed both the House and Senate in June 1906.

Mancos watched all this with great excitement, convinced that the community would benefit immensely. The editor of the *Times-Tribune* (May 18, 1906) saw nothing but prosperity coming with the park's arrival: "This means that the government is going to spend thousands of dollars building roadways, making the park easy access for visitors, cleaning and beautifying the park, constructing hotels and drilling artesian wells." All this would benefit Mancos and the region with the resulting publicity and "will necessitate the expenditure of a considerable sum of money for this part of the country."

The paramount development the editor wanted was a "first class hotel" to handle the onrushing tourist trade. Once it was built, tourists would unceasingly come for fishing, hunting, boating (where, he did not say!) and "other pleasurable amusement." Possibly a sanitarium might be built for health seekers. With its dry, clear climate and lots of "ozone," Colorado enjoyed a statewide boom of sanitariums for the "one-lunged army" and other sufferers during those years. Mancos would finally reach the "promised land."

The editor warned his readers on June 15, however, that it was not all up to Uncle Sam. Although Mancos had fertile land, first-class water "and lots of it," plus timber, coal, stone, gold, and "splendid scenery and climate," that might not be enough: "Let us remember that cities are made, not grown, and the making depends upon the citizens themselves."

That sentiment expressed well the expectations and hopes of an isolated part of the state that had never enjoyed a sustained boom or had much expectation of ever having one. The promised moment loomed at hand. President Roosevelt signed the bill, and finally after a decade-long struggle Mesa Verde National Park became official on June 29, 1906.

The secretary of the interior would control the park, and "all prehistoric ruins situated within five miles of the park boundaries" would also be under the "exclusive control" of the secretary. Creation of the park service was still a decade in the future. Meanwhile, the secretary was authorized to permit examination, excavation, and other gathering of objects, provided they were always "undertaken only for the benefit of some reputable museum, university, college, or other recognized scientific or educational institution." To ensure that nothing else was done, anyone removing, disturbing, destroying, and "so forth" the ruins, graves, and relics would "be fined not more than $1,000 or imprisoned not more than twelve months."

Victory had been achieved, but what, at the moment of victory, had

happened to the women? They had laid the foundation, educated, organized, lobbied, written, lectured, refused to accept defeat, and raised funds,
but in the final stretch most of them remained strangely on the sidelines.

At this hour of triumph, the association had split into two factions.
Discerning folk could have seen it coming. Two women—the equally
strong-willed, determined, and independent Lucy Peabody and Virginia
McClurg—had pledged themselves to a common cause in saving Mesa
Verde. They had worked zealously and doggedly, yet they could never com-
pletely contain their individualism and their different ideas.

Peabody had always supported the national park plan, whereas McClurg
lent her support reluctantly, after circumstances forced her to do so. In her
heart, she supported a park controlled by the women who had fought for
and won it. She would then have more control over "her" park, for which
she had further plans. Sadly, a rivalry existed between the two communities
involved—McClurg represented Colorado Springs and its interests, and
Peabody came from Denver, which had its own agenda. Each hoped to
gain from being *the* successful backer and, concurrently, each wanted to
gain an advantage over a rival.

These tensions had always lurked beneath the surface and the two leaders had their supporters. A few indications had surfaced previously, but not
until February 1906 had they reached the press. The *Pueblo Chieftain*
(February 13) told its readers that "serious controversies" had arisen and
divided the women. The clash between McClurg's women's or state park
and Peabody's national park factions came into the open. The split was so
serious that the *Durango Democrat* predicted at its February 21 meeting,
the association would divide, "and the indications are that Mrs. Peabody
will win." The *Denver Times* (February 25) announced that Peabody would
resign at the April meeting to work in support of the national park bill.

Meanwhile, the *Denver Post* (February 23), although praising McClurg for
her work and saying she should always be remembered, chastised her for her
narrow outlook. The cliff dwellings "belong to the world" and were of too
"big an interest to put in the exclusive custody of any single organization."
The editorial concluded with a large dose of truth and a pinch of sarcasm.

> In fifty years from now who will care or know anything about the
> Cliff Dwellings Protective [sic] Association? In fifty years from
> now if the government of the United States takes care of those
> Cliff Dwellings, the whole world will know of them.

The association tried to counter these reports by claiming the dissen-
sion was "entirely without foundation." The story, obviously sent out by
Peabody or her supporters, reported that the Colorado Cliff Dwelling
Association wanted Mesa Verde under its control just as women "had kept
Mount Vernon." McClurg rallied her forces to meet this challenge and at a

meeting in Colorado Springs they endorsed the plan. She wanted to "manage [Mesa Verde] according to feminine ideas." That, in itself, displayed the tension and dissension. Nevertheless, the hope of altering the course of developments came far too late to gain acceptance. The national park idea won handily.

The fight between the two factions became personal, thus ending any hope of compromise. Poor Representative Hogg got caught in the crossfire. The McClurg faction was not happy with him, because they believed he had failed to include all the cliff dwellings in his bill, which was true, and had pushed for national control: "[Hogg's] backbone belongs rather to antediluvian dinosaurs than to modern legislators." Also, they thought he had supported the women's park idea and betrayed it.

An angry and somewhat frustrated Peabody, through the *Denver Times* (February 25), warned about the attempt to put the park under women's control.

> The action of the Colorado Cliff Dwellers Association [the official name was the Colorado Cliff Dwellings Association] however, may result in the defeat of this bill as well as the one that proposes to put it under feminine and individual control and the state may be left in the lurch.

She was right. The issue had grown beyond the association. It had become a state issue, as other towns and people hoped to benefit economically. National interest grew as well, because the sites represented a national heritage. The women's success had put McClurg's cherished dreams in a bind.

The *Rocky Mountain News*, February 13, supporting both the national park idea and Peabody, fired at McClurg saying the "meat in the coconut is that [McClurg] is loath to relinquish the prestige she has gained by reason of her . . . preserving these ruins." The paper and McClurg's opponents argued that "no volunteer association of women can care for and develop" Mesa Verde. McClurg responded, expressing resentment of the "slurs" and the attack on the women's group by the "penny-a-liners" press. Although she praised Peabody and others for their excellent work, McClurg accused them of wanting the Utes removed so they could seize their land. Peabody may not have desired that, but many southwestern Coloradans did. Some of them may have supported the park concept with that idea at least in the back of their minds.

This infighting and rivalry saddened park advocates and may have delayed congressional approval, but fortunately it did not stop it. The accusations, half-truths, and mudslinging sullied the final moments of the park campaign. McClurg won the immediate battle over control of the association, but Peabody won the war. After she resigned, taking her supporters with her, McClurg had complete dominance over the association and its plans. That hollow victory rested uneasily. She no longer had a say in Mesa Verde's future.

McClurg never really changed her belief that the women should control the park as they did Mount Vernon, although obviously the two scenarios were not the same or the heritage comparable. McClurg denounced the federal control that undermined her dream by putting the park in the hands of faceless bureaucrats in far-off Washington. What had they done to preserve the ruins? McClurg argued rather unconvincingly that Mesa Verde would "not thrive" under either state or federal control. After losing the fight, she continued to work toward her goal, advocating that her husband be made the first permanent park superintendent; she lost that battle also.

Lucy Peabody, having worked and lived in Washington, clearly did not share McClurg's feelings or fears. More experienced at working with and within the government, she saw many benefits coming from federal control. She continued to support the national park concept publicly, pointing to Yellowstone as an example of what direct federal government supervision could accomplish. The two views proved irreconcilable. It was Peabody who looked more clearly into the future. That future belonged to Washington and federal control. It would be up to them to chart the course of Colorado's first national park.

The group that stayed with Peabody contained many of the women who had worked so hard and loyally over the past decade. They included McNeil, Thatcher, Summer, and Whitmore. McClurg's supporters came mainly from Colorado Springs.

Edgar Hewett later remembered those days. "It was a notable fight—a regular knock-down, drag-out affair," and Mrs. Peabody went to Washington "to wage it and achieve her objective." He told Jesse Nusbaum that Ella McNeil "supported Mrs. Peabody's fight, if he remembered correctly, along with her group." Archaeologist and longtime Mesa Verde superintendent Jesse Nusbaum, in fact, highly praised McNeil for her work on behalf of the park. "Mrs. John McNeil of Durango, Colorado, and her group of prominent members, representing the interests of the local Mesa Verde region, significantly strengthened Mrs. Peabody's leadership and campaign."

Hewett had been doing more than simply sitting on the sidelines. He "supported and assisted Mrs. Peabody's plan" and sent her "letters advising her as to moves, etc." Nusbaum, who knew many of the people in this drama, further explained Hewett's role: "Dr. Hewett, then employed by the Bureau of American Ethnology, advised and supported [the group] from the sidelines while maintaining friendly relations with Mrs. McClurg's faction." Nusbaum credited the "aggressive" leadership of Lucy Peabody, combined with "her supporting faction," as contributing "importantly to achieving congressional legislation for establishment of Mesa Verde National Park."

Thus ended the noble dream amid recriminations and sorrowful days. The women had won and lost, all at the same time. Whether happy or sad, the women had still won a major victory. As Shakespeare wrote in *Henry VI*:

> Long since we were resolved of your truth,
> Your faithful service and your toil in war;
> Yet never have you tasted our reward . . .

4

THE FIGHT
NEVER ENDS

T he park fight was over, but not the fray between the rival factions. They fought over the fact that Peabody's choice for superintendent had won. McClurg, you might recall, had supported her husband for the position. When she moved the annual meeting to Colorado Springs, the Pueblo group marched out. The large core of Durango women, who had so eagerly and determinedly worked to preserve Mesa Verde, departed when McClurg embarked upon her Manitou Springs cliff dwelling fiasco (see Chapter 5). One unidentified member lamented "that women interested in these affairs could descend to such petty bickering." They had, and continued for years ahead.

Virginia Donaghe McClurg ca. 1890s.

Undaunted, McClurg took it upon herself to interview the man chosen as the first superintendent, Hans Randolph, ostensibly on behalf of the association. Why? "To ascertain whether he would be, in the opinion of that body, a suitable custodian of Mesa Verde." A most amazing interview took place in Randolph's Denver home on August 8, 1907. The reported conversation was based on McClurg's recollections, which may or may not be the most accurate story.

She asked how he had gotten his appointment, and whether he had visited Mesa Verde. Randolph's reply must have startled her: "I've never been there yet, but I know the maps." What caused his interest? "I like adventure." He asked, "What do you call your Association?" To which McClurg, after giving its name continued, "Oh, Major! You must look a little into our work and our New York and California chapters' work." Seemingly, Randolph did not appreciate her group's effort, the reality of which must have startled McClurg.

Then the discussion became heated when McClurg inquired if he would be willing to take the superintendency under certain conditions and made her power play: "The president [Theodore Roosevelt], Major Randolph, has sanctioned our Association's being consulted in regard to these matters; how would you like to have a board of women to promote local interest?" According to McClurg, she told Randolph, "you were a brave man to be willing to take that place with 150 women 'looking on'."

"I do not care about women," he replied. "I've heard things about your Association, but [I] do not take sides." Continuing, his comments deteriorated further in McClurg's opinion: "I always say what I think and I would not like it. [I] do not want anybody spying around. If they come down, I'll be pleased to show them through my park." One can imagine McClurg's shocked expression at the reference to *his* park!

To her credit she pushed to have relics remain at Mesa Verde. Commenting on early archaeologist Jesse Fewkes and others taking "curios and the results" of excavations to Washington and museums elsewhere, McClurg firmly stated: "I wish we could save them for Colorado." Randolph won no points with his response: "Oh! It does not make one bit of difference to me what he [Fewkes] does with the things when he digs them out. I do not care where he takes them to."

As might be imagined, the conversation did not end on a high note: "Well, Major, if you do not want a committee of women, I really must go, as I'll miss my train." McClurg did invite him to see "my Indian room; it is full of interesting things from the Cliffs." She also invited him to come to Manitou as well and visit the "restorations of the ruins" there. What Randolph thought of this interview went unrecorded.

McClurg may have been trying to make a point, that her husband was more knowledgeable than Randolph. To the superintendent's credit, he had high aspirations for what he planned to accomplish at Mesa Verde.

> I expect to make it a fine park and to report solely to the department in Washington. I am going to excavate those ruins, build roads, build a house. I have not much time before winter, $7,500 isn't much money to do [anything] with. Next year, I hope to get a big appropriation for me to work with, something worth while.

That "big appropriation" never came, and Randolph lasted only four years as superintendent. An "out and out" political appointment (which he was), as Jesse Nusbaum called him, Randolph tangled with local businessmen, was accused of financial irregularities, and could not put to rest an "excessive drinking charge." The superintendent was dismissed in April 1911. The reasons given at the hearing included neglect of duty, misappropriation of funds and the use of government money for private purposes. It would be nearly a decade before a trained archaeologist became superintendent.

The fact that Lucy Peabody had supported Randolph did not gain her points with Nusbaum: "Unfortunately, the prestige thus achieved by Mrs. Peabody as an aggressive leader was later offset to a large degree by her unwise choice of superintendent and his ensuing administrative record." So both of the "movers and shakers" had their mistakes along with their obvious contributions.

Recalling these years later, McClurg mentioned something that had not previously been obvious in the breakup of the association: "We have had our troubles. There was an effort to introduce Democratic politics into the

Association, but that was all settled long ago, and we are 'one for all, and all for one'." Earlier, she had commented that the association had "good Republican women," when she was trying to induce Randolph to let them have their say in park matters.

The stress over the park seemed to change McClurg, or caused personal characteristics earlier kept in the background to rise to the forefront. For example, she started talking about having visited Mesa Verde in 1882, something she had not mentioned in the 1889 *Great Divide* articles in which she claimed she had first visited the region in 1885. The earlier date would give her prior claim over those of anyone else, including the Wetherills. Indeed, in her first article (March 1889) she praised the stalwart Wetherills, calling Mrs. Wetherill "a sweet gentle-voiced Quakeress." She characterized them as part of the pioneers, who were the "dominant white race and again the desert shall rejoice and blossom as the rose." Her favorite cliff dwellers had the same qualities.

The forthright, enthusiastic young lady of the 1880s had become a headstrong, embittered matron who wanted center stage for herself and her dreams. The disappointments of the early years of the twentieth century had taken their toll. After all her determined work and the time she spent, McClurg's dream of "her" park had come within her grasp, then fleetingly slipped away. She never recovered from that disappointment, although she stubbornly continued to hope and even scheme.

The bitter infighting must also have hurt, lasting as it did for decades. McClurg eventually "edited" her records to reflect little about Peabody and the "rebels." All told, getting so close to her prize, then seeing her aspirations vanish, had been too much. So much had slipped away, and so many dreams had died with the dawn of the park era. It all had to have been traumatic.

McClurg and Peabody advocates praised their personal heroines and criticized their rivals. McClurg lost out everywhere except among her diminishing group of loyal partisans. With their luster fading and their contributions being forgotten as the park surged ahead, McClurg fought tenaciously to maintain her reputation and the association's. Under her leadership, the association made one more positive contribution to "their" park. They raised a thousand dollars to restore Balcony House, which McClurg had visited many years before. Young archaeologist Jesse Nusbaum, under Edgar Hewett's direction, repaired the ruin in 1910.

The last hurrah came while Americans fought in World War I, a time when the world was changing dramatically from the days when the women had started their crusade. McClurg wrote, planned, organized, customized, and directed a pageant. "The Marriage of the Dawn and Moon" was based, McClurg said, on an old Hopi legend. An effusive reporter from the *Durango Democrat* (September 5, 1917) praised the production: "Mrs. McClurg's pageant is founded on an ancient mystical and romantic legend

The plaque that caused a "flap."

bringing out prominently the prayers of these ancient people, born of the wind and rain, whose father was the sun and whose mother was the earth." Once again, the regent general of the Colorado Cliff Dwellings Association held center stage.

She wanted to be sure the public knew about her contributions. As the *Democrat* told its readers, McClurg "was the first white woman to explore the cliff dwellings, the discoverer of Balcony House, and [the person] who more than anyone else has popularized the story of this earliest recorded peoples." McClurg gave some credit to her husband and daughter-in-law, who "ably assisted." J. Allard Jencon, "a student and field archaeologist as well as musician," wrote the music for the pageant, served as stage director, and played the "role of 'Dawn Light' who married 'Moon Maiden,' the heroine of the pageant."

Performed in Spruce Tree House, with most of the cast of twenty-five "men, boys and girls" from Mancos, the entire performance was filmed to be "shown in thousands" of theaters across the country. Following the most "pretentious pageant" ever undertaken in Colorado, the guests sat down to a banquet of roast calf, roast sheep, baked ears of maize, and trays of peaches. McClurg designed this menu to reproduce the Indian "staples" of the region. Whether the movie in reality proved a great advertisement for Mesa Verde National Park, as hoped, has been lost to history along with the film. One of the movie "directors" remarked that with a "little more time devoted to practice, the pageant would make a great success."

The Durango newspapers gave the best coverage of the event, with no mention of the need for more "practice." The *Herald* (September 10) hailed "Mrs. McClurg to whom belongs chiefly the credit for staging the

Virginia McClurg's pageant makes its debut.

pageant." The reporter was also impressed by what he had learned. "From the presentation it is apparent the ancient cliff dwellers believed that evil spirits lived in the underworld and good spirits were found in the heavens."

The *Democrat*, September 5, 1917, had a much longer and scintillating review, which began:

> While California has had her Mission Play, unique among the sisterhood of states, Colorado's story is that of the most ancient Americans, the pre-Columbian cliff dwellers, and yesterday its first dramatization and presentation in Spruce Tree House ...
> [the reporter went on to assert]
> Many of the tourists acclaimed the poetry and music of the pageant as a literary event of historical and scientific interest. Never in the state history or in the West has a more beautiful and mystical early historical drama been presented.

McClurg could not have written it better herself.

Wartime limitations and changing public tastes, however, doomed "Marriage" to history's dustbin, a forgotten relic of yesteryear. Nothing seemed to commemorate, or even recall, the association. The pamphlet, "A Summer Outing Amidst the Cliff Dwelling Ruins," published about the same time as the pageant, showed photos of some of the things they had

Colorado Historical Society

"Marriage" lasted one performance.

accomplished, including the restored Balcony House, but nary a mention of the women. McClurg still did not give up. After getting a second wind and recovering from illnesses, she wrote National Park Service director Stephen Mather a long typed letter. It revealed much about her and her attitudes as of 1920. Earlier she had sent him photographs of her Mesa Verde pageant.

These photographs are, I think unique, in that they show a theatrical event (my own dramatization of an Indian legend) costumed, drilled, enacted, with dances and songs, by twenty-four actors, without cost of admission, staged in ruins, forty miles from nowhere, and in the midst of a population which— but as they are your Park constituents—I draw the veil.

Her bitterness toward local people must have reflected what she perceived as their failure to follow her lead fifteen or so years earlier.

She regretted not having gotten on with her plan before now, but World War, her illness, and the influenza epidemic had prevented it "so that we are just now able to take up our labors and need some special work to reawaken interest." Referring to the association, she reminded Mather that "several years ago our society repaired Balcony House at our own expense." She went on to claim, "This is the ruin my party discovered Oct. 4, 1886."

What the association "would ask is that you permit us under the Government to control this ruin and install therein a *field* museum, with perhaps one room devoted to *case* museum objects, from the Pueblo Indian Southwest, and Mesa Verde in special, free to the public." She pointed out her own "fine and comprehensive" collection, indicating she intended that some of it would be placed in Balcony House "under certain conditions." She truthfully praised the Colorado Cliff Dwellings Association for its work and for saving what it had. McClurg went into some detail about what they had done and did not leave herself on the sidelines: "I have a letter from former President Roosevelt, our friend and helper, saying 'Mrs. McClurg's society should be recognized in the administration of the Mesa Verde Park.'"

McClurg, with her usual enthusiasm and aplomb, opened her last paragraph with a ringing promise:

> I feel confident we could make our Museum a centre round which we could gather a summer session of ethnologists and scientists, nature lovers and tourists for Mesa Verde Park. What Enos Mills and Mrs. Sherman have done for Rocky Mountain National Park, we could do in even greater measure for such a park as Mesa Verde. There need not be any expense for the Government, about a museum at Balcony House, save transportation and service connected with that and the right to have a camp near by, for the persons connected with the museum only.

With that out of the way, she had a complaint. When "we repaired" Balcony House, the women understood that the government would build steps of native rock "to give safe and easy access to Balcony House." That had not happened. "Instead, a most hideous and dangerous perpendicular wooden ladder was installed—obscuring the face, and a terror to the arm-chair ethnologist." She wanted "safe and easy" access to be the "best example of *finished* architecture in the Mesa Verde region." So have many visitors since!

Mather replied on June 16, opening politely and carefully: "I am in full sympathy with your organization and the work it is doing, and none has a higher appreciation than I of its efforts in behalf of Mesa Verde National Park, and it is my sincere hope that they may continue." He then went directly to her request and concluded by describing the role of national parks.

> Because of this it makes it doubly hard for me to say, after carefully considering your proposition from various angles, that I can not consistently give it my approval in just the form which you have brought it before me. I most certainly would welcome the opportunity to have the Association perform additional constructive work in the park, but frankly I could not grant it special privileges in the way of control in any sense over any part of the ruins. I think you will appreciate this point of view when I add that the national parks are created for all of the people, without reservation, and it is the duty of the National Park Service, as custodian, to administer them in this manner.

It is doubtful that McClurg appreciated that point of view at all.

Balcony House which the women helped preserve.

Mather correctly worried about the precedent that would be set by the women having control over any of the ruins or park exhibits. He did, however, encourage McClurg to donate "the many objects [of] which you speak," which would be a "welcome addition to the park's museum." The director closed by expressing hope that the association would "continue to cooperate in advancing the interests of the park."

Not completely finished, the association reappeared again the next year. In 1921, Nusbaum—now the park superintendent—found at the Mancos railroad station a crated white marble marker that commemorated McClurg's and the association's contribution to the park's development. McClurg made one last effort, pressuring the National Park Service to install the marker "in the most conspicuous location for visitor observation" at Balcony House. The unfortunate Nusbaum found himself in the middle of what quickly became and remained an emotional issue.

The Peabody faction soon learned about McClurg's effort and argued that other leaders merited equal recognition with her. If the monument flap had been allowed to continue, Mesa Verde might have ended up like some Civil War battlefields, with monuments to almost all those who had "fought" there. Fortunately, it did not. The Park Service discouraged such commemorations at Mesa Verde, and McClurg, once again faced with opposition, backed off. The marker was returned to Colorado Springs. That ended McClurg's efforts, but it did not end the "cause."

Jesse Nusbaum seemed haunted by this dispute. Years later, shortly after McClurg's death, her friends made another attempt to commemorate her at the park. He remembered that the campaign was "vigorously renewed in June and July 1931, shortly following Mrs. McClurg's death, when Mrs.

Visitors stop for a meal.

Maude Price, Regent of the Colorado Cliff Dwellings Association, sought permission on behalf of the Association to place a bronze tablet on Balcony House commemorating the achievements of President General Virginia Donaghe McClurg." The Park Service rejected the idea.

The association then recommended placing a tablet in the museum. That request went no further. Price received a letter from the secretary of the interior stating that, "placing a bronze tablet on the Balcony House [or museum] would not be in keeping with the policy of the Park service or this department." The women did gain a small victory, as Nusbaum later recalled, during yet another flap over the issue: "These episodes were eventually closed by giving a brief mention of the work and contributions of Mrs. McClurg and the Colorado Cliff Dwellings Association in our park information leaflet."

Even that small tribute eventually disappeared, and the women drifted further into the dark recesses of forgotten history. Despite declining in numbers each year, they did not forget, but rather awaited another day.

Peabody's faction fared no better than McClurg's. Her supporters wanted Square Tower House renamed Peabody House, which it had been called unofficially. That request spurred angry protests and letters from the McClurg contingent, and the Department of the Interior, fed up with the whole thing, rejected the designation. It also did not want to establish a tradition of naming ruins. The idea did not die, and Peabody's supporters awaited a better time and another opportunity.

In 1946-1947, another attempt was made to pressure the superintendent to rename Square Tower House the Peabody House. Acting Superintendent (both during and shortly after the war) Jesse Nusbaum had been down this road before and did not relish retraveling it. Regrettably, he had to. Peabody's friends reminded him that it had originally been called Square Tower, then briefly, in the 1910s, it had been called Peabody House. One of them wrote, for example, that Peabody had spent her "own money and time," until they had saved the ruins. Now no one "knew what she had done."

It was Hewett who had changed the name of Square Tower House to Peabody House. Although Nusbaum "did not know the facts of the case," he understood "that, in response to protests, the Department of Interior rejected Dr. Hewett's Peabody House designation." He went on to state:

> At the time Dr. Hewett redesignated this cliff dwelling as Peabody House, park travel was practically negligible, as the area could be reached only by horse trail. Then, outside of Nordenskiold's notable report and a few minor reports, there was so little literature relating to the park to fix the name of Square Tower in the public mind, that a change in its name at that time would have caused only limited confusion. However, since 1908 nearly 450,000 visitors have entered Mesa Verde and most of them have visited this cliff dwelling and know it as Square Tower House. Save for brief mentions of Peabody House in an article or two by Dr. Hewett, the name of Square Tower House has since that time become so firmly fixed in the public mind through all park and other publications, including Dr. Jesse Fewkes' "Excavation of Square Tower Ruin," that it appears inadvisable to change a name that has been regularly used for fifty-six years.

In a memo of February 5, 1946, Nusbaum laid out what he considered appropriate reasons for naming unnamed ruins after a person or an organization. This should be done "only where the contribution is so outstanding and significant as to engender universal recognition and support."

If, he argued, a ruin or natural feature was named after Peabody, "friends of other deceased individuals could rightly claim a comparable recognition." One person had already suggested that Mrs. John McNeil had earned "equal recognition in establishing the park," therefore, why not honor her?

Nusbaum concluded, "Because of the appropriateness of the name of Square Tower House and the prestige of long use and association, I recommend that the original name, Square Tower House, be perpetuated without change." He did not do this out of disrespect for Lucy Peabody: "I make this recommendation without prejudice whatever to Mrs. Peabody's important contributions to the establishment of Mesa Verde National Park."

Mrs. Alicia Irvine, who apparently instigated the renewed push to honor Peabody, did not stop with the superintendent. From her Denver home she wrote to members of congress, the regional director of the National Park Service, and the Department of the Interior. In August and September 1946, she received two replies from the Park Service Director that should have put the matter to rest.

This Service fully appreciates the untiring efforts and significant contributions that Mrs. Peabody made in behalf of Mesa Verde National Park, and careful consideration has been given to your suggestion. We believe, however, that any departure from established policy would bring a flood of similar requests, not only at Mesa Verde but at other areas administered by this service. (August 9)

Except in very special cases, it is contrary to National Park Service policy to change names that are fixed in an area through publication, long use, and association in the public mind, and it is not customary for the Service to recognize the contributions of individuals by naming places or objects after them. This policy applies whether the persons be distinguished men or distinguished women. We do not feel that the policy is a hardship on park benefactors because such persons are motivated by the impulse to save or help save some outstanding part of our national heritage for future generations of Americans and [they] pursue this ideal for its own sake. (September 20)

Those clear statements should have ended the matter for the ages, but Irvine carried on the struggle into the 1950s, when, finally, no more letters appear in the park archives. The tempest passed for the last time; the original participants were either gone or elderly, and the bitter sparks barely glowed.

The park had been created forty years before, and neither side had the numbers or the determination to carry on the fight any longer. Sadly, because of all the bickering and pressure, the Park Service decided not to honor any of the women. Thus, their story remained largely unknown for another generation.

What had started with such enthusiasm, high expectations, and dedication came to this dismal end at the start of a new era. Colorado had changed, America had changed, and the world had changed since McClurg and Peabody started their crusades generations earlier. As the Jazz Age had replaced the sentimental ballads of the 1890s, and the toe-tapping ragtime melodies after the turn of the century were supplanted by Elvis Presley and rock and roll, so had Mesa Verde changed.

Although the Park Service knew about the women's role, the public did not. That slowly changed, however. On the seventy-fifth anniversary of the park's creation, a press release hailed it as the "only national park created largely through the efforts of a private group of women." Since then, more attention has been paid to the women, the start of long overdue recognition.

At the same time, women's roles at the park also expanded. There had been women archaeologists, interpreters, and seasonal employees earlier, but it was not until 1973 that the Park Service hired a woman ranger. Mesa Verde now marched with the rest of the country in giving women the opportunities their abilities should have gained for them years before.

5

SAD AFTERMATH

F rom the apex of her triumph, a discouraged, disgusted Virginia McClurg had seen her dreams crushed long before 1921. Mesa Verde would not become a state park, her husband would not be superintendent, the now splintered Colorado Cliff Dwellings Association would no longer be a major player at Mesa Verde, and she found herself at odds with her longtime associate Lucy Peabody and her supporters. Meanwhile, the park progressed without her guidance. The situation must have been frustrating for this strong-willed, activist woman.

McClurg had been the major player in making the public aware of Mesa Verde, organizing support for saving the ruins, and planting the idea of a park. But sadly, she could not enjoy the moment of victory. Her association was split and feuding; she was on the sidelines and there seemed little she could do to mend the rift. Nevertheless, she hit upon a way to reinvigorate her dream and control its destiny.

Courtesy Denver Public Library

**Virginia Donaghe McClurg
ca. early 20th century.**

Earlier, while McClurg was still somewhat involved with Mesa Verde, she had made a fateful, foolish decision. If she could not dominate the destiny of the park, she could at least help create her own cliff dwellings and guide their fortunes. By making that choice, McClurg left an unwanted and unwarranted legacy for the national park, one that relentlessly bounded down the decades, a hound chasing a shadow of what might have been.

That decision definitely impacted her reputation and her rationale for preserving Mesa Verde, tarnishing, though not completely overwhelming, what she had accomplished in the past decades. It was regrettable it happened at all, but understandable for this domineering, headstrong, determined woman who had grown to consider cliff dwellings her special project to be kept under her guidance and control. Her reputation, though, never fully recovered, and her fake cliff dwellings in Manitou Springs, Colorado, bedeviled several generations of park superintendents and employees.

Unfortunately, they also fooled tourists and promoted a false image of the cliff dwelling era. Edgar Hewett summarized the impact clearly. After failing to "have her husband, Gilbert McClurg, appointed to the Superintendency, [McClurg] promoted the construction in a natural cave at Manitou, Colo. . . . of an assembly of fake Mesa Verde Cliff Dwellings—advertised in such manner for some years as to mislead the

Fake "cliff dwellings" at Manitou Springs.

MANITOU SPRINGS

The famous showman P.T. Barnum is credited with saying, "There's a sucker born every minute." The public can be gullible and be taken in particularly if the attraction appears easy to reach, well promoted, and does not involve much effort to understand.

For more than ninety years, these observations have been precisely what worried Mesa Verde personnel about the Manitou Springs "cliff dwellings," which had, and have, no basis of fact in that canyon location or general locality. Their promoters—intentionally or not—misled the public into believing that they represent the "real McCoy." Barnum, whose popular American Museum was based on the public taste for humbug, would have understood completely.

uninformed." Those years stretched into decades.

She had not originated the idea. It belonged to "professor" Harold Ashenhurst, head of the Ashenhurst Amusement Company. In November 1906—Mesa Verde's first year as a national park—he and others incorporated the Manitou Cliff Dwelling Ruins Company. Apparently, criticism arose early. An article in the *Montezuma Journal* (November 29) stated that the company had no intention "of trespassing on Mesa Verde." It was, the company stoutly declared, "a misapprehension to suppose that any attempt was being made to remove ruins from government ground." The promoters intended to reproduce "Cliff Palace, Lone Tree Balcony and Kodak Ruins" from material gathered from "patented ground and . . . purchased from ranch owners."

A young, self-promoting Texan, Ashenhurst had "excavated" a valley site ruin (later identified as Blanchard Ruin) on private land south of the town of Dolores. W. S. Crosby, one of the company's incorporators, had "secured most of the relics to be had" in Cortez, claimed the *Montezuma Journal* (October 25, 1906). Crosby continued to be a hit with the paper and local residents. He went on to say that "they [incorporators] expect to spend six thousand dollars among our farmers in getting them to the railroad." Piously, he noted "these ruins are some scattered over this valley, the ones in Mancos canon belong to the government and will not be touched, but will remain to attract tourists as of old."

He pointed out in an October 25 interview what example the owners planned to follow with the new cliff dwellings. Referring to those Mesa Verde sites mentioned above, Crosby went on to explain, "It is from a blue print of these" that he and his associates "intend to erect their facsimile in the canon near Manitou." What did they plan to do? "Take stone from scattered ruins over this valley . . . and rebuild them in the mountains near [Colorado Springs], and charge admission."

Throughout the first half of 1907, the collecting and buying went on with vigor. The company trail can be traced in comments from the *Montezuma Journal*.

> Hauling of the Aztec ruin rocks still continues, they being shipped to Manitou, where the Mancos canon ruins are being duplicated. This enterprise is distributing considerable loose change in this valley. (February 21, 1907)

> This Association has gotten many Aztec and Indian relics from this country for their reproduced Cliff house at Manitou. These curios will increase in value as years go by, and will always bear the records of an ancient history as they are now doing, and are rapidly becoming few in number. (April 25, 1907)

> Adam Lewey hauled some figured Aztec rock to the Dolores depot this week for shipment to Manitou. Parties are reproducing these ancient ruins in a canon near that place. (May 9, 1907)

Someone on the paper staff had a sense of humor. On June 13, this gem appeared, referring to Adam Lewey, who had been doing much of the collecting as well as purchasing some of the relics from the locals.

> Mr. Lewey will take his family up to Mesa Verde soon, and about the first of the month will go to Manitou, where rumor has it that he will disguise himself as an ancient Aztec, and direct attention of visitors to the imitation Cliff ruins now being reproduced there. It is a sure thing that Lewey could tell them as much as anybody about those old time castles.

The work went on well into 1907, with more than forty carloads of what had been found, mostly stones transferred to the Rio Grande Southern depot at Dolores and shipped from there. Eventually, everything reached Manitou Springs, the mineral springs neighbor of the tourist Mecca, Colorado Springs. This also placed the new cliff dwellings virtually in McClurg's backyard.

Not everyone was happy, despite the money coming into the area. It seemed to some that a heritage was disappearing. They hoped a national park would bring in more money over time. Harkening back to the *Journal* of February 21, 1907: "The D.& R.G. are widely advertising these Mancos canon ruins and many tourists will arrive there this season to see the genuine article."

The association did not get everything. In October 1906 the Guillet brothers sold their collection "of Aztec pottery to the State Agricultural College." According to the *Journal*, "they had a very fine array of these prehistoric relics, and the price, two hundred and forty dollars for a hundred and twenty pieces, was certainly very reasonable." It certainly was; that amount represented a fair income for farmers and ranchers in Montezuma County. Crosby arrived just two hours too late with his offer to buy the collection.

Safely out of the way of criticism from southwestern Colorado and archaeologists elsewhere, Ashenhurst and Crosby busied themselves planning and constructing a cliff dwelling ("two-thirds original size") at the "head of beautiful Phantom Canyon" in 1906-1907. Ashenhurst had McClurg's blessing, along with that of the Colorado Springs faction of the forsaken, depleted association. The association had busily raised money to purchase relics and Navajo blankets "for their reproduced Cliff house at Manitou." McClurg became interested in Ashenhurst's idea after she lost the park fight, control there slipping from her hands, and while the association also floundered in the press and among many of the interested public. She became a company stockholder, a foolish if understandable action. Unfortunately, McClurg's support gave the scheme a semblance of credibility that Ashenhurst, stingingly called a "medicine show operator," never could.

Criticism of the plan grew almost as quickly as the new cliff dwellings went up. The Colorado Society of the Archaeological Institute of America made a "vigorous protest." The *Rocky Mountain News* (November 16, 1906) concluded that "troubles like evil birds are hovering" near the Ashenhurst company and "its pet scheme" of building a copy of Cliff Palace in Dead Man's Canon.

This was the final straw in many people's minds. Wrote one unnamed poet:

> Sing a song of science, the science of a cliff,
> Forty resignations of women in a tiff;
> When her mail is opened and the regent notes the row,
> Won't she be disgusted by the "quitters" final bow?

The article went on to state that "forty of the leading members" of the Cliff Dwellers' Association resigned. "These resignations form a sequel to a volume of disapproval brought out by Mrs. McClurg's action last summer," when she appointed a committee to "confer with Mr. Ashenhurst." The "scheme smacked of commercialism and did not appeal to the Denver and Pueblo members." They felt "that there had been an end of the whole matter when the national park" had been created. McClurg did not agree.

More women resigned from the faltering association, leaving McClurg in control again. It proved a Pyrrhic victory. One reporter wrote, the association "will be even less substantial than the crumbling ruins for the preservation of which it is alleged to be devoted." Even Ashenhurst betrayed her in the end. McClurg had only wanted the little cliff dwellings to be an imitation that would interest visitors who could not undertake the "arduous" trip to Mesa Verde. Ashenhurst had other ideas about his project's future.

Initially, McClurg and Ashenhurst advertised their cliff dwellings as a reproduction, but that notion quietly faded away. The Manitou Springs site seemed much more attractive and convenient for travelers who did not want to brave the poor roads, mountain passes, arduous driving, and days of traveling it took to reach Mesa Verde from eastern Colorado. Thus, Ashenhurst came to promote Manitou Springs as the "real McCoy." Like carnival barkers, the company turned its spiel to what the public wanted to hear. Ashenhurst, in it for the money, went his merry way. The short- or long-range impact on the park and on archaeology did not appear to matter to him.

Even McClurg began to have second thoughts, or perhaps she was trying to keep the association from losing further members. In a late 1906 letter to member Sarah Decker, she explained her position and what had happened.

> Why has the [Cliff Dwellings Association] been cursed up and down the State in the journals and by the club-women, because it gave Mr. Ashenhurst a "hearing" upon his cliff-dwelling canon reconstructions?
> I did not summon Mr. Ashenhurst to the platform; he was simply permitted to tell the ladies of his plan between sessions. . . The lies about this Ashenhurst matter are thicker than "Autumn leaves that strew the brooks of Vallambrosa" but these are the facts,—let any one who can, disprove them.

She went on to say, "I have not *one cent* involved in any proposition of this kind," adding that the association "has no interest in Mr. Ashenhurst's proposition and probably never will have." McClurg and several others had gone up the canyon to look at what was happening, and she felt deceived by what she saw. "He invoked the aid of the Association to supervise his restorations and direct that they be done scientifically, and not as a fake show." The entire story of Virginia McClurg's involvement with Ashenhurst may never be known. That she played a role in the Manitou Cliff Dwellings, particularly in the beginning, cannot be questioned. That she was completely honest in telling about her involvement can be doubted, or perhaps she convinced herself of what her role, or lack thereof, had been. Newspaper accounts of the same period contradict her story, but their complete reliability can also be questioned, depending on the source they used.

Meanwhile, the Denver & Rio Grande railroad and others were "widely advertising" the Manitou Springs ruins, and visitors started to come. Before many years, Manitou seemed to rival the park. The public in the 1910s and 1920s was not yet going on long trips by automobile because of the inconveniences involved, including few good roads, unknown accommodations, and lack of information. Taking the train to Colorado Springs seemed faster, easier, and much more familiar even if old-fashioned. The trip offered more tourist attractions than one to Durango and Mancos, and even when they arrived at the latter, travelers still remained, at best, hours away from the park.

Mesa Verde did not appreciate its fake rival. Jesse Nusbaum, the park's first trained archaeologist superintendent, had a multitude of problems in the 1920s, most of which were left over from earlier years and political appointments. On top of this, McClurg's Manitou Springs fiasco haunted him endlessly.

An earlier pamphlet advertising Manitou Springs had boldly stated that "everyone knows prehistoric Cliff Dwellers lived only in the Four Corners, a region even now difficult to access." The writer was honest enough to describe Manitou Springs as a "reproduction" but then went overboard, claiming it was an "exact and scientific reproduction." For the small admission of one dollar, one gained "easy access" and a "courteous guide to conduct you through the ruins." What must really have annoyed Nusbaum was the inclusion of a letter from him discussing the cliff dwellers but not the Phantom Canyon fake, thereby potentially implying his endorsement of the Manitou Springs "ruins" to the uninitiated reader.

Nusbaum expressed his true feelings in a letter he sent to the director of the National Park Service on March 21, 1924. He exploded:

> Each year, I get more "Red-Headed" than ever, when visitors to the Mesa Verde later visit the fake Cliff Dwellings at Manitou, and return to me the folder received with their comments thereon. They say imitation is the sincerest form of flattery—but a fake is a fake and should be so proclaimed.
> I resented their reproduction even under the original plan, long before I became superintendent of this Park.

Guides, he told the director, led visitors to believe: "Why visit Mesa Verde when you can see it all here for a dollar?"

He resented not only the fact that the Manitou dwellings were fake, but he resented their impact on the park: "It really works a great hardship on this Park to be forced to compete with such a combination," and their constant "'Bally-Hoo' near a great tourist center like Colorado Springs."

Although the advertisements were "not nearly so bold and brazen as they were in the beginning," Nusbaum had had enough. He wanted the government to prosecute the owners of the Manitou Springs Cliff Dwellings for fraud. Unfortunately, after government inspectors gave the matter "careful consideration," they wrote him that the charge of using the mail "to furtherance a scheme to defraud" could not be proved with the evidence submitted. They concluded: "It is regretted that the matter does not appear to warrant further attention."

In the same March 1924 letter, Nusbaum told of an attempt to trap the Manitou proprietors. Two years earlier, he wrote, the proprietor and his wife had announced that they were going to Mesa Verde to excavate "for a month or six weeks to gain new material for their museum." A friend in Manitou tipped "me off regarding their plans." The Park Service employees awaited their arrival and recognized them, even though they "registered in from Rock Springs, Wyoming." Nusbaum assigned a ranger to watch "them so closely" that they "evidently gave up their quest." The disappointed superintendent concluded, "They were given several fine chances to 'start something' in the excavation line if they dared do so, but I guess that they knew their game was up."

That game was up, but the misrepresentation and competition were not. Superintendents who followed Nusbaum continued to be plagued by false advertising and misinformation comparing the park with the "wonders" of Manitou Springs. Besides the fact that the Manitou dwellings were a fake, Nusbaum and others faced the reality that southwestern Colorado remained isolated. The remote park seemed to have little to offer compared with Colorado Springs, its famed nearby mountains, and other attractions along the Front Range.

The 1930s depression cut into long-distance travel to Mesa Verde, and the rationing of gas and other staples did so even more during World War II. It wasn't that Manitou Springs did not still aggravate; other problems simply pushed it to the sidelines. The potential for more trouble loomed on the horizon.

Train travel had dropped off steadily in the 1920s and 1930s, replaced by automobile travel. With the end of World War II, Americans took to the road as never before. Thanks to rationing, shortages and overtime in the war years, people had saved money. With the return of peacetime, more opportunities existed to buy new cars. The interstate highways were making travel easier and faster, and accommodations—from motels to restaurants—multiplied along America's roadsides. Towns promoted themselves as tourist havens and people were interested in visiting them. All this promised better days for post-war Mesa Verde.

However, the decades-long "civil" war between the park and McClurg's "museum-quality" Manitou Springs Cliff Dwellings simmered on, seemingly interminably.

In July 1946 Superintendent Robert Rose discussed the decades-old problem of misinformation given out at Manitou Springs. With Americans traveling again, Colorado had become a choice destination. Colorado Springs, with its many attractions, was one of the most popular sites. Many travelers had never been West before and believed what "informed" locals related to them about these "real" cliff dwellings and the "Anasazi" who lived in them. Unfortunately, to the uninformed, it sounded believable.

Visitors to Manitou were "told that it is very difficult to get to the Mesa Verde ruins," an obvious contrast with the ease of reaching theirs which were just a short drive out of Colorado Springs. Not always mentioned but implied without question, the national park was found "away down" in the isolated southwestern corner of the state and time-consuming to reach. According to the Manitou Springs folk, it was necessary to "ride horseback many miles over poor trails" to reach the cliff dwellings. To make matters worse, the park had "no guides." One could easily imagine getting lost in the wilderness! The obvious conclusion: Why travel to Mesa Verde's ruins? They "can't compare" with Manitou Springs!

Rose reviewed "the many attempts that had been made in the past by Mesa Verde personnel to minimize or correct this situation." Sadly, he concluded, "little had been accomplished other than to prevail" on the Manitou folks to develop "less brazenly misrepresentative advertising." The increasing possibilities for advertising during these years only made matters worse.

The private owners continued to represent the "fake ruins" as genuine: "Evidently their oral advertising continues as unscrupulous as ever. Of course, persons who subsequently come to Mesa Verde 'see the light.'" It was from those people and from letters that the park continued to hear about the goings-on at Manitou Springs.

Meanwhile, the real story of the Manitou Springs Cliff dwellings was not revealed. The facility continued to receive acclaim it did not deserve. *The Colorado Year Book 1962-1964*, in the section on Manitou Springs, contained this priceless gem about the Phantom Canyon display: "Archaeological preserve dating from 1019 AD," displaying homes, weapons, burial urns, and other artifacts of a vanished civilization. The ghost of Virginia McClurg must have laughed.

Mesa Verde archaeologist Jean Pinkley, a woman pioneer who arrived at Mesa Verde in 1939 as a museum assistant, did not laugh. She wrote the Rocky Mountain AAA about their 1964-1965 issue of *Where to Vacation in Colorado*. This publication included much of the same misinformation that the yearbook contained. The furious, outspoken Pinkley pointed out the obvious: cliff dwellings never existed in eastern Colorado. Not stopping there, she continued, "Reproductions are not an archeological *preserve*." These "pseudo-cliff dwellings duplicating sections of Spruce Tree House, Cliff Palace, Balcony House and Square Tower House were first advertised as reproductions." Pinkley did not hesitate to sharply point out that "through the years any intimation of the buildings being reproductions was dropped."

She had "made a very thorough inspection," along with other archaeologists, and they had all concluded: "Not only are they fakes, poorly constructed fakes at that, but the self-guiding panel exhibits in place are full of mis-information, some of which is actually ludicrous." The same held true for the "so-called museum" included on the site. It was, Pinkley bluntly informed the AAA, nothing but a "tourist-trap."

Whether this impressed the publication's editor is unknown, but it unequivocally represented the decades-old frustration of the people at Mesa Verde over McClurg's misguided legacy. Slowly, though, times were changing. The public was becoming more informed, more aware, and, it is hoped, less gullible. Despite the continued claim of "museum-quality" exhibits, the Manitou Springs fake, at least, trapped fewer people. Still, they could not accomplish much to stop the fraudulent exhibit.

Times did not change completely, however. The decades went by, and Manitou continued to promote its cliff dwellings. People kept coming and being taken in by what is a poor reconstruction at best.

There has been less trouble between the park and the privately owned cliff dwellings recently than there was in the past. Both recent park superintendents, Robert Heyder and Larry Wiese, said they have had no dealings with Manitou Springs. Nor did the park receive a significant number of complaints or concerns from tourists. No attempt has been made to curb the private enterprise. It does generate a certain amount of revenue for its local area, as Mesa Verde does for southwestern Colorado. To have the federal government step in would probably arouse sympathy, particularly in El Paso County, with its well-known objections to any federal intrusion into private enterprise.

This lack of friction does not necessarily mean the two facilities have reached their angle of repose. The pseudo-cliff dwellings live on, and now, in the twenty-first century, they are promoted on their website. The messenger might be new and up-to-date, and bring the message right into your computer at home or at work, but the message is as old as McClurg's initial involvement. It does rather remind one of the carnival barker's pitch to the crowds on the midway.

> The Manitou Cliff Dwellings is [sic] a rare historical treasure. Preserved under a protective red sandstone overhang, authentic Anasazi cliff dwellings, built more than 700 years ago, await you

here. There are no "Do Not Touch" signs. You are free to touch and even go inside these fascinating architectural remnants of an American Indian culture that roamed the Four Corners area of the Southwest from 1200 B.C. to A.D. 1300.
Take a trip into America's past. Plan to visit the Manitou Cliff Dwellings soon.

It is hoped not too soon!
Continuing on through the message, it invites one to tour everything else with one exception: "it isn't appropriate or possible to go down into the kiva." Is it not possible because none was blasted out back in 1906-1907? Certainly, a visitor can climb down into one at Mesa Verde or Aztec Ruins without arousing the wrath of the ancient gods.
The 2004 website does not stop with this come-on; it continues to lure the unwary into the tourist trap.

These authentic cliff dwellings were first opened to the public in 1906. Since then we have taken great care to preserve them so that generations of visitors can travel through time to experience a great American society now long gone. [As you explore each room], we invite you to imagine what it was like to live over seven hundred years ago in a structure like this. You can even have your picture taken in front of a building that's a lot older than your Grandfather!

Whether it would be "a lot older" than one's grandfather would depend on whether that grandfather was alive in 1906-07.
The website "surfer" next reaches the question-and-answer section. Out pop gems such as this: "Can I buy Indian artifacts? Actually, buying ancient Indian artifacts might get the Antiquities Police on your tail, and you wouldn't want that to happen would you?" Fortunately the Antiquities Police do not mind of course, if you buy a souvenir or two in the "well-stocked" gift shop.
The tourists today might be wiser, yet they still succumb to the old carny's pitch. Making a profit is the goal, without concern for any "Antiquities Police." Ashenhurst's ghost lives on in more than memory in the twenty-first century.
Fliers and pamphlets available at the Manitou Cliff Dwellings are more circumspect and just as blatantly misleading as the Internet site. For example, the visitor is invited to "wander leisurely" through "these actual ruins (c1100-1300 A.D.). . ." and "perhaps you can even 'feel' the spirits of the people who lived, worked and communed in such spaces centuries ago." A short pamphlet, *The Manitou Cliff Dwellings Museum,*" is more truthful. It states the "original stones were acquired from McElmo Canyon in Southwestern Colorado and brought to Manitou through the efforts of

concerned and interested citizens." Great pains are taken to emphasize the "museum" makes "examples of cliff dwellings easily accessible to the public." Interestingly, no mention appears of Virginia McClurg or any of the people who created the attraction.

It was advertisements and promotion like this that upset Nusbaum and the professional park superintendents who came after him. Despite everything Mesa Verde has done, and the fact that the public is better educated today about the ancestral Puebloan people, Manitou Springs cliff dwellings endure. It is not the memorial Virginia McClurg and those women who worked with her would have wanted.

Mark Twain, who fortunately never visited these deviously deceitful cliff dwellings, explained clearly why they continue to attract the gullible and the naive: "The history of our race, and each individual's experience, are sown thick with evidence that a truth is not hard to kill and that a lie told well is immortal." Twain, whose love of cats was legendary, explained it another way: "One of the striking differences between a cat and a lie is that a cat has only nine lives."

"IT IS SAD INDEED THAT MANITOU SPRINGS REMAINS PART OF HER LEGACY..."

One might optimistically assume that Virginia McClurg would not have wanted the Manitou Springs cliff dwelling exhibit to end up this way, although some people who worked with her on the project would not have been astonished at all at such a result. She might have been bitter; she might have been distressed over her failure to control the destiny of the park; but she had tried to preserve the prehistoric treasure of Mesa Verde as honestly as she could within the limits of her generation. Unfortunately, her Manitou Springs venture turned out less favorably, albeit profitable for the owners.

It is sad indeed that Manitou Springs remains part of her legacy, in direct contrast with her positive contributions and those of her followers in southwestern Colorado. Like the park, the Manitou reproductions are approaching their 100th anniversary, reaffirming what Mark Twain observed. The English poet and playwright William Shakespeare wrestled with the same problem on several occasions. In *Julius Caesar,* during the funeral oration for the late emperor, Mark Anthony intoned these immortal words.

The evil that men do lives after them:
The good is oft interred with their bones.

SOMETHING
OF WHICH TO BE PROUD

By the 1920s, tourists enjoyed a "cleaned up" park.

O ne can be truthfully amazed at how fleeting was the fame of the women of the Colorado Cliff Dwellings Association. The fact that their contributions have been generally forgotten should not diminish all that the women accomplished in a relatively short time. Few of them did it for glory and fame. The preservation of the sites and the creation of a national park presented enough reward for their efforts.

"...FEW PLACES OFFER SOMETHING AS EXTRAORDINARY AS MESA VERDE."

Their heritage of saving and developing Mesa Verde into a national park lives on. Many more visitors now arrive in a week in the summer than would have come in a year during the early days. Tourists appeared in increasing numbers once the roads improved and the mountain passes became more manageable for flatland drivers. Then airplanes made access even better. And visitors continue to come, not just from nearby states but from throughout the world, to see a legacy that is not America's alone.

Women tourists savor "their" park.

Thanks to these women's initiative, Mesa Verde was launched on its way to becoming a world cultural heritage park. Perhaps they dreamed that something like this would someday occur. They made the park more accessible and more tourist friendly and successfully publicized it in a variety of ways. No doubt much to their satisfaction, the mesa and cliff sites are now strictly guarded and preserved so that generations to come may have the opportunity to visit, study, and enjoy the park.

Lucy Peabody discerned all this when she predicted that thousands would come, which meant hundreds of thousands of dollars would pour into the state and the region annually. She challenged Coloradans to "turn their backs upon seductive watering places in the East or the attractions of Europe."

"Take an outing" to Mesa Verde, she advised.

She was right. The park has garnered not thousands of dollars but millions annually for the region, state, and nation. That does not include the publicity and fame that have come with having such a storied attraction in the neighborhood. The park has given southwestern Colorado something special to lure tourists. Spectacular mountains, impressive plateaus, and beautiful river valleys can be seen elsewhere, but few places offer something as extraordinary as Mesa Verde. In total, it has proved a nearly irresistible attraction.

The women's efforts also sparked interest in saving other cultural sites, as well as in creating national parks and monuments that were ultimately preserved under the federal shield. Archaeologists and other researchers have benefited immensely from the women's efforts and the example they set in their fight for the park. The secrets of the past have been, are being, and will continue to be unlocked, thanks to those determined women. It is hard to imagine what might have happened had they not stepped up to the plate.

Virginia McClurg and Lucy Peabody, despite their later differences, could take pride in what they accomplished. McClurg, because of her post-park actions, received less favorable publicity than Peabody. As one of her partisans wrote, though, her "interest never flagged," and Colorado had a national park due "in largest measure to her patient, continuous and self-denying work, covering a quarter of a century." Peabody's followers also were correct in pointing out that "no woman in the country has a more thorough and profound knowledge of archaeology." The "earnest, able and enthusiastic" woman, through her "untiring efforts," to a "great measure" accomplished the national park goal.

Peabody hailed and thanked Edgar Hewett for "rendering invaluable service." She praised his "skilled and unfailing assistance," which did more than "any other thing to preserve the ruins at Mesa Verde." The other women and the men who joined the movement should not be forgotten. In their own way, each caught the vision and contributed to the eventual success of the cause.

Notwithstanding these contributions, a sadness lingers in this saga, woven into the very fabric of the women's story. The clash of personalities, the divergent paths toward preservation of this irreplaceable heritage, and frustrated dreams led to the division between leaders and their followers on the threshold of victory. Neither side appeared able to forgive or forget, then or later. Bitterness haunted the story of the women at Mesa Verde for

THE QUARTER

When the United States Mint announced it was going to honor each state with a statehood quarter, much discussion occurred as to what Colorado should place on its quarter. Starting in 1999, each coin would appear in order of its statehood date with five coins issued every year. Being the thirty-eighth state (1876, hence the nickname the Centennial State), Colorado had some time to make a decision.

Mesa Verde quickly became a popular choice in southwestern Colorado, but other sections had their own favorites. The result was a decision to send five designs to the Mint which then would make the final selection. Mesa Verde made the cut, and it will be a fitting tribute if the park is selected.

Tourists at Mesa Verde could send postcards home.

another generation, hindering the telling of the tale and preventing others from gaining a complete appreciation of what they accomplished. Perhaps they should have read more seriously Alexander Pope's admonition: "To err is human, to forgive divine."

No matter the personal clashes, these women symbolized their generation's involvement in the world beyond the home. In their way, they contributed to the women's movement solidly taking root throughout the United States, as the young twentieth century gained maturity. They had to overcome female stereotyping and become directly involved in the men's world of politics, activism, lobbying, and even business. They did all this and more, and they succeeded in achieving their prime objective.

All of them should be hailed as the mothers of Mesa Verde. We also must not forget the men who worked with them on a variety of tasks and who followed the women's lead. The entire group, spearheaded initially by Virginia McClurg and then joined by Lucy Peabody and the others, saved the ruins for posterity. They took the gem of an idea about preserving America's prehistoric heritage and turned it into something alive, something vital. That dream lived beyond them. Their example stimulated interest, helped educate the larger public, and brought others into the movement.

There may have been a national park eventually without their efforts, but how much more of Mesa Verde's material heritage would have wandered away, been lost, stolen, or destroyed if more time had slipped away before that day came and people acted? How much longer would it have taken to educate and energize the public and politicians? How much longer would it have taken to generate enthusiasm about preserving other sites and enthusiasm for preservation in general? The answers will never be known, but the women and their supporters made these questions academic because of their success at Mesa Verde.

Lucy Peabody understood their contributions. She affirmed that the "state has something of which to be proud." Not only the state but the nation, and beyond those to the world, can be proud that the past has been preserved for the future. In a favorite expression of their day, "three cheers and a tiger" for the women of Mesa Verde. They can all be hailed as Mothers of Mesa Verde.

SUGGESTIONS FOR
FURTHER READING

For those interested in delving into Mesa Verde's fascinating story, the following books are suggested:

Mesa Verde Shadows of the Centuries, by Duane A. Smith, (Boulder: University Press of Colorado, 2002) provides the general overview, as does *The Story of Mesa Verde National Park*, by Gilbert Wenger, (Denver: Mesa Verde Museum Association, 1980). *Those Who Came Before*, by Florence and Robert Lister (Tucson: University of Arizona, 1983) and *Trowelling Through Time: The First Century of Mesa Verdean Archaeology* by Florence Lister (Albuquerque: University of New Mexico Press, 2004) are fine places to start. *The Cliff Dwellers of Mesa Verde*, by Gustaf Nordenskiold, (Glorieta, New Mexico: Rio Grande Press, 1979 reprint) puts the reader back to the 1890s.

For those who wish to research deeper, the libraries of the Center of Southwest Studies, at Fort Lewis College, in Durango, Colorado, and Mesa Verde National Park are fine places to start. The Colorado Historical Society and the Denver Public Library also have a variety of Mesa Verde material.

INDEX